The Resourceful History Teacher

Also available:

Jane Martin: *Women and the Politics of Schooling in Victorian and Edwardian England*

Robert Phillips: *History Teaching, Nationhood and State*

John Slater: *Teaching History in the New Europe*

Lez Smart: *Using IT in Primary School History*

The Resourceful History Teacher

JOHN LELLO

CONTINUUM

London and New York

To the many students of all ages who have shared
a love of history

Continuum

The Tower Building
11 York Road
London SE1 7NX

370 Lexington Avenue
New York
NY 10017–6503

First published 2001

British Library Cataloguing-in-Publication Data
A catalogue record for this book is available from the British Library.

ISBN 0–8264–5124–1

Typeset by YHT Ltd, London
Printed and bound in Great Britain by TJ International, Padstow, Cornwall

Contents

Introduction

I asked some 10-year-olds in a primary school in Bridport, Dorset what they thought history was. One said it was Granny; another said it was the church; a small girl at the front said it was Snow White. So I asked what they would think if Snow White met Granny in the church, and the little girl at the front said that she thought it would make a good story. They were beginning to explore the kind of evidence that was within their experience. They were at once making connections and considering actively what the subject was about. They had not met me before so I thought it useful to try what has been known in some quarters as a David Sylvester. I threw my wallet on the classroom floor and invited groups of three at a time to find out things about me from what they could extract. 'You are very rich,' said one, on seeing two five-pound notes. 'You belong to a swimming club,' said another, 'so you must be fit.' 'Here is a dry-cleaning bill, and you should have collected the suit yesterday.' After half an hour they knew a lot about me and they had handled and touched a considerable amount of material and had interpreted much of it fairly easily. They would have continued for some time but already they knew a lot about this man who had walked into their territory.

History is about using evidence, about variety in content and exposition and about telling a story. In the 1960s, Bloom used the word 'taxonomy'; a familiar designation in natural history, which came from two Greek words: *taxis* meaning order and *nomos* meaning a law. He wished to describe a structure that categorized and classified the laws and principles of education. He distinguished between the affective and cognitive paths to learning. His taxonomy became fashionable and was taken up by Coltham and Fines who used it to demonstrate how it related to the study of history. Others, like Sylvester and Booth, were didactic and tried to encourage children to discover things for themselves. There were not, however, two rival camps but two contrasting and complementary ones; one was trying to

THE RESOURCEFUL HISTORY TEACHER

delineate the character of history and the other was exploring the way history could be taught.

The Schools Council History Project, developed by Sylvester and his team, emphasized a skills-based approach and stressed the centrality of evidence. It soon became as fashionable as the Bloom taxonomy. Many of the ideas from the Schools Council Project, concerning the place of evidence, were incorporated into the new GCSE examination that was introduced in 1988. This was a replacement for both the CSE and Ordinary Level exams and catered for the whole range of abilities that had been tested previously by two separate exams. There had barely been time to adjust when the National Curriculum was introduced.

This major educational reform, introduced in 1991, was highly prescriptive in content and increased teachers' teaching and administrative hours. Historians were required to give pupils a broad chronological grasp, an approach intended to be a corrective to the earlier skills-based pattern of 1988. More changes were to come.

Political correctness had had a powerful influence on history teaching during the nineties. The demands, for example, of ethnocentricity (regarding one's own race as more important) left many teachers confused or feeling guilty. Confused because many of the existing printed materials had a British slant and were therefore very difficult to use, and guilty because for some the new political correctness involved the rejection of long-held customs. It thus became a question of what it was possible to teach with confidence and fairness. For example, is it 'correct' to be as open and unbiased towards an orthodox Islamic or Marxist regime as it is towards one of the systems of proportional representation?

Gender issues were also critical areas in the teaching of the 'new history', not because the facts are hard to handle but because of the emotive postures that surround them. Many such attitudes are embedded deeply in any person's psyche and many of these sensitive issues, and others like slavery, poverty, globalization and constitutional reform, deal with areas of controversy.

In the end, much of history teaching is shaped by the attitudes of the teacher. The frankness of a discussion about feminism, say, in a university seminar will not be mirrored in the way many teachers, of either gender, teach in a school classroom.

Attitudes, inevitably, pervade education generally and history teaching in particular. They become the bedrock of the way we teach and of the content of our teaching.

This book includes a range of topics that are meant to contrast both in content and method but which are not meant to be a comprehensive survey. The subjects included are intended to contrast with each other (e.g. comics and Charlemagne), and the hope is that teachers will feel encouraged to explore new ideas, even within the limitations of the curriculum. The topics also offer a chance to question personal attitudes and to investigate why one may, for instance, have a reaction against the current interpretation of social Darwinism or the teaching of the history of costume. In short, the topics aim to be a representative survey.

The book is certainly concerned, therefore, with the place of attitudes in the learning and teaching of history. Attitudes are an inescapable part of our lives, not only because we are historians and are involved in the way people, including ourselves, think and react, but because we have lived at a particular time. Our own context in time – when we were born, where we lived and how old we are – is the key to our lives and we cannot escape it. It is also a major factor which governs our personal attitudes. It is impossible for me to forget that I was a child in east London during the blitz and was evacuated to an uncle in Radnorshire. The blitz, and the evacuation, may not have been pleasant but they have made an indelible impression on my life. When I read a book about Hitler I think about the rich language of my father as he retreated to an Anderson air-raid shelter because a young airman from Germany was dropping bombs on our street. When I read a book about the Industrial Revolution it is impossible for me to ignore the visits to Lancashire mills which were part of my earlier life as a teacher in the North West. The pain and deprivation of the history of that industry I have always seen in the context of the noise, the banter and the general good humour of the mill floor. When I think of the Industrial Revolution I think not only about the spinning jenny, but also about another Jenny who swore like a trooper and made me laugh as I looked at her working at the machine. My point is, simply, that all the research in the world is not going to change my attitude to those things which are part of the context of my life. It is important to recognize, therefore, that these are the parameters within which I will teach.

Kurt Hahn, who founded Gordonstoun School and was the educational midwife for the Outward Bound schools and Atlantic College, said, on opening the latter, that he did not believe it would be possible to remove prejudice but that we should learn to live with it. Learning to live with prejudice was not only one of the guiding principles of that educational visionary, but should also be one adopted by the history teacher.

During the 1970s there was much discussion, in the Stenhouse Schools Council Humanities Project, about the possibility of being a neutral chairman. This proved to be a difficult role if the teacher was to have a significant input and not allow external elements to dictate the proceedings. The essential premise was that the teacher should stimulate a student discussion with a film or a recording and then

temper the ensuing controversy with dispassionate, impartial comment. However, there is a difference between being unbiased and
being clinically neutral. In several parts of this book I suggest that one
possible approach, in some topics, is to have the two separate sides of
a question represented by two contrasting people or teams. This can
be a useful approach but it does mean that the teacher should be ready
to redress any imbalance on one side or the other, and should the
teacher have to do this he or she should exercise care.

This introduction has touched upon some recent trends in the
teaching of history, but there are older and much deeper philosophies
mentioned under the headwords in this book. The substantial or
speculative, the analytical or critical and the narrative are three
commonly accepted groupings of historical philosophies, but whatever
the category, all philosophers deal with the same questions: What is
the nature of history? Can a course of events be explained? Are
general laws possible? Is history cyclical? Can we learn anything from
history? All the philosophers would give different answers to these.
Marx would see the course of history as a class struggle with material
objectives; Toynbee would seek to explain history though a series of
cycles and with a scientific approach to human affairs; Kant sought to
detect a purposive interpretation; Collingwood thought that the
reconstruction of thoughts – 'to inwardly re-enact' – would help us
understand human actions. What they do not tackle is the question of
how we *learn* history. This is a modern question.

Fifty years ago history teaching would have been chronological,
factual and would have comprised a tight narrative. Some of it would
have been learned by rote, some through dictated notes or by intensive reading, and all students would have been tested regularly in
order to ascertain how much they had absorbed. Nowadays the
teaching strategies are not so straightforward nor so uniform. Teachers today would not be so single-minded about purely factual learning.
Some would feel that the student should learn how to use evidence
and compose and defend a rational argument and should show an
appreciation of past achievements. All this, they would conjecture, can
enhance the syllabus of the National Curriculum.

We learn history by using as wide a variety of methods, styles,
sources and techniques as possible and we should, therefore, aim to
offer as many contrasting forms of presentation as possible. It is sad
when some of the old methods are neglected or allowed to lapse
merely because they are old, when they can still be effective. We do
well to remember that the object of the exercise is not to impress
students with the most up-to-date machinery but to discover the best
ways in which they can learn.

Methods of teaching history fall into four categories and each entry
in this book falls into one of them. The use of *machines* in teaching

history is the first category, and in recent years it has been augmented greatly by the development of Information Communication Technology (ICT). This label covers a range of innovations that are becoming commonplace to more than just the 'enthusiasts'. The range of web-sites, CD-ROMS and the like enhance, enrich and enable. However, they are expensive to buy, date rapidly and consume teaching time with a vengeance. It is impossible to live without ICT but it does need to be managed carefully, more so than most tools. The list of head-words relating to machines also includes films and film strips, gramophone records, radios as well as a battery of support under the headword **classroom aids**.

Action is the second category, describing entries like trips, visits and the like. The development of such activities has burgeoned since the introduction of the National Curriculum of which they now form a part. One has only to go to the British Museum, or indeed any museum in the country, to see the way in which much educational use is made of what is available. There has been a spark of interest from schools and colleges and this, in turn, has brought about a plethora of activity by the museums, which have improved greatly as a consequence. This improvement of the presentation of existing artefacts has been due mainly to the efforts of English Heritage and the National Trust, both of whom have been able to use lottery money. The museums them-selves have also been challenged by having to decide whether it is helpful, as well as being permissible historically, to develop and display their artefacts more imaginatively, or whether to leave them un'enhanced'. It is like the dilemma faced at Knossos, on Crete, when Sir Arthur Evans and M.S.F. Hood had to decide whether to leave the ruins as they found them, or whether to reconstruct them. They decided on a partial restoration. Faced with such dilemmas, British museums have made a variety of different responses: the York Castle Museum stayed the same as it had always been whereas the Yorvik museum in the same city, decided to create a wholly new experience. Tower Bridge remains an interesting monument in its own right, but inside, a reconstruction using 'virtual reality' makes one feel alive to what happened in the same building many years ago. Teachers must decide which type of visit is more useful for their needs.

The third group of methods in teaching history concerns those which relate to the *spoken word*. An unattainable but useful rule is that the teacher should never talk for more than ten minutes without introducing something by way of contrast. This may be as simple as a picture, a sound tape, an artefact or a document. Classroom teachers need to beware of talking too much and should remember that the attention span of any student is limited. A high intelligence does not always guarantee a greater capacity to concentrate. A common mis-take committed by a teacher is to become excited by the subject and to get 'carried away'. Enthusiasm is, of course, valuable but it becomes a hazard if all the other rules are disregarded in the process. I suspect that many students have enjoyed the fact that their teacher loves his or her subject, but they do not always remember what the enthusiasm was about. 'I remember when you talked about Welsh castles and your eyes were ablaze with the images you were creating; I can still remember your eyes.' It is perhaps a pity that the student could not remember anything about the castles. The process of teaching is of little value unless it enables *learning* to take place. However, one cannot be too prescriptive about teaching technique and, in particular, the technique of telling a good story, which is especially relevant to history teaching. Some gifted people can bring a subject to life by teaching it with colour and sensitivity, and we should not be too quick to impose rules concerning the length of time a teacher should speak. The ten-minute rule is just a guide.

Finally, there is the *written word*, especially important because history is a literary subject. This book deals with documents, legislation, newspapers, worksheets and books. The problem for history teachers is that there is so much material. The answer is that whatever is available should be easily accessible, perhaps in the form of a classroom resource-centre library or a card index listing all the materials in the school or college relating to the subjects being explored. Whatever the method, the accessibility of the written word is paramount and should always be so. There is nothing more off-putting than to find that the very document that would further research in a particular subject is not readily available, particularly when it means that a luke-warm student loses interest, when it has been hard to arouse his or her interest in the first place.

As well as the four categories cited above, this book also includes a series of topics in history, which are not meant to be a history of the world but which serve as illustrations of the ways in which contrasting topics can be approached. These topics include biographies of individuals such as Marx and Mill. They include philosophies, such as *laissez-faire* and mercantilism, and they include umbrella topics like historiography and political philosophy. All of these, and others, are meant to be illustrations of the kinds of topics which lend themselves to a range of different approaches.

In addition, there are some craft 'rules' which are meant only for guidance, but which should remind the teacher of the key maxims that are worthy of respect, even if they are not always adhered to. There are those gifted practitioners who break all these rules and yet teach effectively and well. Nevertheless, rules and principles cannot be founded upon the practices of such one-off geniuses.

There are seven 'rules'. The first of these is to use a *variety of methods*. This ensures that the student gets the point. It ensures continued interest and does not permit the mind to wander. It may mean dealing with the same topic using a film, a document, a reading, an essay, question-and-answer techniques, or any other method. Every lesson should contain variety.

The second rule is to *emphasize by repetition*. This is a time-honoured rule, but one which is often ignored. I recall a history teacher who repeated again and again that Saint Augustine landed at Ebbesfleet, Thanet, Kent. At the end of the lesson, which was on the beginnings of Christianity in England, he asked 'Where did St Augustine land?' The whole class was able to write the answer.

The third rule is to *test the old before embarking on the new*. Although this is sometimes a bore, and often disliked by the class, it is a valuable discipline because it means that the students have a foundation for the new material. The forms that this recapitulation can take vary greatly but it need not take long and should not be forbidding nor form the main thrust of the lesson.

The fourth rule is the technique of moving from the familiar to the new. The danger of using this rule is to overuse it, so that the student groans inwardly when the old material is rehearsed. The teacher's skill lies in recalling the old in such a way that it doesn't sound old. Sometimes when the subject is, say, an invention in the Industrial Revolution, it is enough to display a picture of the actual machine or the mill or the people who were most involved in the product's development. What matters is that the subject is recalled quickly. It is easy to forget that a student may have attended several other classes before coming to the history class, and therefore a gentle recap on the previous lesson is necessary to allow the student to adjust mentally.

The fifth rule is for the teacher to *allow time for the material to be understood*. This can mean scheduling in time for reading, writing or preparation. The old method of dictating notes was often criticized for glossing over the material so quickly that there was not enough time for the student to digest it. I have a mental image from the past of a teacher walking about the room, monitoring and guiding, and where standing at the front was apparently achieving very little. The students must have time to think and explore for themselves. This thinking and exploring ought to be part of the learning process and should, consequently, form part of the lesson.

Next, try to ensure that the *old work is really understood* before embarking on the new. This is hard to achieve but it is always worth the attempt. Not all historical subjects require total recall of their foundations, but many do, and it can be confusing for a student if the fundamentals are not secure. The student who has been absent must be able to go over the ground that he or she has missed.

The most important rule is the last: the teacher should try to *ensure that learning history is enjoyable*. Most students – indeed most people

– are fascinated by the subject and will display a genuine interest in what happened in the past. This is because history is part of their own experience. There are several entries in the book like time, family and other such topics, which relate to parents, grandparents and other relations. Few of these subjects are boring for students; start any lesson by mentioning Uncle Joe the fighter pilot, and there is an immediate response. Even though many modern families follow different patterns, an interest in relationships remains a constant. Formal marriage arrangements are nowadays less popular, but their sociological replacements have not caused a lessening of a sense of involvement in the past, or the present. This means that the history teacher starts with an in-built advantage and is able to capitalize on this natural interest in the past. To go around a museum with a group of young people is to have one's own awareness sharpened, and this is not always based upon the kind of interest one would expect. So we learn history by building upon the natural interest in the subject with which we were born.

This book can be used as a *vade mecum* of the possibilities that exist. First, it is arranged so that method entries and subject topics are listed in a single alphabetical sequence. Thus, Napoleon is next to National Curriculum. Sometimes one entry makes reference to other associated headwords, and these are listed at the bottom of the entry, where such references exist. The other means of cross-reference is the index, which lists in detail the places where a particular person or topic is mentioned.

What then is the purpose of this book? It is meant for teachers of students of all ages, including young children as well as adults. It is thus equally applicable to the reception class in primary school as it is to a class in the University of the Third Age. This intentional applicability does not mean that it is a compendium which includes all the material with which to teach the history of the world. It suggests paths that might be constructive to take, but the actual subject material is not included. For example, the entry for Information and Communication Technology indicates what exists, but the entry for Australia only highlights some of the key items that might be considered in the history of that country. Huge chunks of history have been omitted intentionally, because to do them justice would involve providing a great deal more information than this book is designed or intended to provide. It is also meant for teacher trainers as a checklist of the methods they might wish to employ.

I have tried to avoid jargon because I fear it often confuses the reader and, moreover, can be a serious deterrent.

The book is also intended for student teachers, in the hope that they will be encouraged to use all the techniques that are available to them. It is recommended that they read through the *whole* book rather than using it for reference only, in order that they may gain an overall awareness of what is on offer.

These then are the people for whom the book is primarily intended, and the purpose of it is to lay before them the possibilities that exist in the teaching of history. By setting out existing strategies, it is hoped that those who read the book will feel able to try out ideas they have not used before. Paradoxically, although the last 30 years have seen a revolution in the teaching of history, with refreshing approaches to the subject coming into being, in terms of materials and subject matter, the amount of time allocated to history as an obligatory subject in the National Curriculum has been reduced. It is hoped that the perspectives and possibilities suggested herein will not only increase the likelihood of having more history taught in schools and colleges but also of having it taught more effectively.

A

Advanced Level. GCE Advanced Levels (A Levels) are designed mainly for post-16 students who are following a two-year, full-time course of study. A Levels are generally based on six units of approximately equal size. Three of these make up an Advanced Subsidiary (AS) course representing the first half of an Advanced Level course of study. The other three, representing the second half, are known as A2. A Level and AS courses may be assessed either in stages or at the end of the course. They should be seen as an opportunity to increase the breadth of sixth-form studies. In a few small-entry subjects, where the regulatory authorities accept that it is uneconomical for awarding bodies to offer both staged and end-of-course assessments, only the latter option is available. In most of these cases, there is the option of taking the AS halfway through the course.

Assessment. A key feature of A-Level courses has been their emphasis on demanding and rigorous assessment, including a substantial external element. For some subjects with criteria, there has been a modest increase in the proportion of internal assessment (coursework). All A Levels include an element of synoptic assessment designed to test candidates' ability to make connections between different aspects of the subject. The synoptic element must normally contribute 20 per cent to the full A Level and take the form of an external assessment at the end of the course. The nature of the synoptic assessment will vary according to the nature of particular subjects. In line with the intention that A Levels should be, predominantly, two-year, full-time courses, only one resit of each assessment unit is allowed. It is possible to retake the whole examination more than once. The shelf-life of assessment units is limited by the life of the specification (syllabus).

Grading. The A Level will be graded A to E for pass grades, with U (unclassified) for a fail. Formerly, an N grading (near miss) was awarded to give students who had just missed a pass some formative

feedback. There is evidence that this function was not well understood by candidates. It is now unnecessary because units are
separately certificated.

Advanced Subsidiary. The reformulated GCE Advanced Subsidiary (AS) was a key recommendation arising from Lord Dearing's
review of qualifications for 16–19-year-olds. The Advanced Subsidiary consists of three units of approximately equal size which form
the first half of the A-Level course. AS Levels are designed to
support progression and encourage breadth in post-16 programmes.
Those students who, having started an A-Level programme, decide
not to continue beyond the first year with one or more subjects will
have their attainments up until that point recognized. Students will
also be able to use the new Advanced Subsidiary to broaden or
enhance their A-Level studies.

Assessment. The coursework and external assessment requirements for the Advanced Subsidiary are part of the requirements for
the full A Level. There is no synoptic requirement in the Advanced
Subsidiary, but in all other respects – resits, certification and shelf-
life – the Advanced Subsidiary requirements are the same as for A
Level. The material examined in the Advanced Subsidiary is selected
from material examined at A Level. Sample questions are provided
to help teachers understand the requirements of the qualification.

Grading. The Advanced Subsidiary is graded on an A to E scale,
with U (unclassified) for fail. Achievements on the Advanced Subsidiary, and on A2, contribute in equal measure to the full A Level
and provide as great a challenge as former linear papers.

Provision for the most able. The government has announced the
introduction of new 'world class tests', aimed at the most able
students. These will be designed to be more accessible than the
current Special papers.

See separate entry on **Key Skills** under **General National Vocational
Qualification**.

Marshall, B. (1999) 'The measurement myth: how do we assess school performance?' *Education Review*, **12**(2), 53-6.

aerial photography. Aerial photography has five functions in the
teaching of history. It may be used to reveal site and situation or to
demonstrate strategic positions, communications, development patterns or ancient remains and building foundations. Its application is
not limited to any particular historical period. For example, it is as
revealing and helpful to see how Hitler could enter France around
the Maginot Line as it is to see a motte-and-bailey castle in
Berkhampstead or the expansion of Lincoln from Roman times to
the present day. The positions of roads, canals and railways are as

important to our understanding today as they were to bomber pilots finding their routes over Germany in the Second World War.

Aerofilms Ltd (1954) *Classified Index to the Library of Aerial Photography.* Borehamwood, Herts.
Hawkes, J. and Kendall, T. (1999) *London from the Air.* London: Ebury.
Stonehouse, B. (1982) *The Aerofilm Book of Britain from the Air.* London: Spring.

affective learning.   Affective learning deals with emotions, feelings, beliefs, values and attitudes, in contrast to psychomotor and cognitive learning. These qualities were outlined by B. Bloom in *The Taxonomy of Educational Objectives*, London, Longman (1956). They are discussed in detail in P. Lang (ed.) *Affective Education*, London, Cassell (1997).

Agrarian or Agricultural Revolution.   The Agricultural Revolution consisted of a series of major changes in the industry between about 1750 and 1850. It has been argued that it had good and bad effects. Common land was transferred to private ownership, which increased the size of farms, removed usable land from agricultural labourers and made women dependent. The old open-field system was designed for subsistence and involved all members of the family. The restructured system slowly but irrevocably changed the basis of rural society, although the changes were uneven over the whole country.

Jethro Tull, Thomas Coke of Holkham, Robert Bakewell and Arthur Young pioneered innovations in cultivation, selective breeding and drainage. New technologies and machines were also introduced by Andrew Meikle (threshing), Robert Salmon (hay tossing) and Patrick Bell (reaping). All these changes were part of a wider and general reforming zeal. This helped to make farming more efficient but this in turn soon resulted in lower wages and unemployment. Cereal production doubled between 1750 and 1840, but so did unemployment.

See separate entry on **countryside.**

A key text is the eight-volume *Agrarian History of England and Wales* (1986-9), edited by Joan Thirsk, except for the first volume which was edited by H. P. R. Finberg and published in 1972.

Sale, K. (1996) *Rebels Against the Future.* London: Quartet Books.
Snell, K. D. M. (1985) *Annals of the Labouring Poor: Social Change and Agrarian England 1660–1900.* Cambridge: CUP.

American democracy.   A form of government that developed from the American Declaration of Independence presented by Thomas Jefferson, on behalf of a committee of five, during the revolt against

England. It was proposed to Congress by Richard Henry Lee, seconded by John Adams on 2 July 1776 and formalized on 4 July 1776.

> We hold these truths to be self-evident, that all men are created equal, that they are endowed by their Creator with certain unalienable Rights, that among these are Life, Liberty and the pursuit of Happiness. That to secure these rights, Governments are instituted among Men, deriving their just powers from the consent of the governed. That whenever any Form of Government becomes destructive of these ends, it is the Right of the People to alter or to abolish it, and to institute new Government, laying its foundations on such principles and organizing its powers in such form, as to them shall seem most likely to effect their safety and happiness.

It provides the essence of political democracy especially when it is taken together with the Gettysburg Address, given on 19 November 1863, during the American Civil War, by Abraham Lincoln to the Second Inaugural Congress:

> we are highly resolved that the dead shall not have died in vain, that this nation, under God, shall have a new birth of freedom; and that the government of the people, by the people, and for the people, shall not perish from the earth.

Twentieth-century amendments have added important changes for women and blacks. A simulation of the American Congress is helpful and the American Embassy in London is helpful in supplying materials and experienced advisers. They also have a useful resource library.

Garraty, J. A. (1998) *The American Nation.* London.
Foner, E. (1999) *The Story of American Freedom.* London: Picador (from which the following quotation comes): 'The idea of freedom is the revolving kaleidoscope of American society and the prime organizing theme of American history.'

American Historical Association.   Founded in 1884 and has some 16,000 members. It publishes the *American Historical Review*, *Perspectives*, an Annual Report and pamphlets, and runs regular conferences and seminars. It is based at 400 A St S. E. Washington, DC 20003; tel: (001) 202 544 2422; fax: (001) 202 544 8307; e-mail: aha@thea.org; website: http://www.theaha.org/info/index.html

American Museum, Bath.   Depicts the lifestyle, crafts and wars from America's past. It contains a Folk Gallery; the reconstruction of a farmhouse tavern built in 1758 in Pelham, Massachusetts; a large collection of African-American quilts made by slaves on the Mimosa Hill Plantation, Texas; a replica of George Washington's flower garden at Mount Vernon, Virginia and the Dallas Pratt Collection of Historical Maps of the world and western hemisphere. Throughout the summer months the American Museum is host to a number of groups which demonstrate a variety of events from America's past. They vary from displays of native American dancing and eighteenth-century military drills to re-enactments of fighting in the French and Indian Wars and the American Civil War. Educational tours are available regularly (provided notice is given in advance) and there are also tours of the garden in the spring and summer.

Calverton Manor, Bath, is signposted from the centre of Bath. Tel: 01225 460503; education: 01225 463538; fax: 01225 480726.

anthropology.   The study of human beings, societies and customs. It includes the links with forbears and involves the concept and science of evolution. The latter is particularly useful in teaching the development of earlier civilizations. It is useful to the historian because it can allow direct observation of features and customs which have left little evidence. The classic text is *The Origin of Species*, written in 1859 by Charles Darwin (1809–89). He explains the development of the species by natural selection which automatically weeds out the less fit and results in the 'survival of the fittest'. There is also a useful direct comparison with the selective breeding of cattle which played such a significant part in the agrarian revolution of the eighteenth century. 'Man with all his noble qualities . . . still bears in his bodily frame the indelible stamp of his lowly spirit' (Charles Darwin, *The Descent of Man*, 1871).

See separate entry on **Darwin**.

Barfield, T. (ed.) (1997) *Dictionary of Anthropology*. Oxford: Blackwell.
Desmond, A. and Moore, J. (1991) *Darwin*. London: Michael Joseph.
Mead, M. (1962) *Male and Female: A Study of Sexes in a Changing World*. Harmondsworth: Penguin.

It is also helpful to consult the Natural History Museum which has a good education section. It is excellent on anthropological questions.

archaeology.   The study of remains, monuments and antiquities. Because the core of archaeological discovery is by excavation and primary research, it is a valuable way of introducing students to the raw materials and essential roots of the past. For example, a Roman road not only imparts wonder and excitement but also reveals part of the very substance of history at a critical and, usually, early stage of learning.

The modern interest in industrial archaeology makes every town a source of interest and every child a useful researcher. At Iron Bridge in Telford, Shropshire, UK, children are actively involved in running the small town that they have helped to restore as a working museum.

A form of intellectual tourism is currently popular and consists of highlighting the cultural values of an area by organizing heritage theme parks or open days in any building that is usually closed.

Several pamphlets are available from English Heritage:
Archaeology in London (1997) (XH20037); Coastal Archaeology (1996) (XH10877); Industrial Archaeology (1995) (XH10822); The Management of Archaeological Projects (1991) (XH20007).
Clark, G. (1965) Archaeology and Society. University Paperbacks. London: Methuen.
Greene, K. (1983) Archaeology: An Introduction. London: Batsford.
Lavell, C. (1997) Handbook for British Archaeology. Edinburgh: Edinburgh University Press.
Renfrew, C. (1996) Archaeology. London: Thames and Hudson.

archives.   Historical records or documents which provide part of the raw materials of history. They will always be limited in their scope because they relate to a specific time, like the Battle of Britain, a specific place, like the cathedral at Truro or a specific person, like Prince Albert.

Two main difficulties are, first, putting the records in their correct context and, secondly, in their correct relationship to the whole; for example, the significance of Napoleon's death within the contexts of his own life, the development of France and the development of Europe.

Most British counties have an archives office with a valuable store of primary documents which can often be photocopied and used in class teaching. These offices also have publications which relate to local history, sometimes prepared especially for children.

See separate entry on **county record offices.**

Emmison, F. G. (1966) Archives and Local History. London: HA.
West, Joan (1971) Archives for Schools. London: HA.
West, Joan (1992) Classroom Archives. London: HA.

architecture.   The science of building. It is one of the physical records of human achievement and a reflection of lifestyle, through the planning of such matters as space, heating and ease of main-tenance. It is an expression of thoughts and values; for example, building a spire which points to the heavens or an open-plan office which enables everyone to see what everyone else is doing.

Types of buildings reflect many aspects of society and often involve the use of local materials. One example of this is the construction of houses using wattle and daub. This consisted of daubing mud and animal hair over chestnut hurdles which were supported by wooden posts set in stone feet. Another example is cobb shattering. This was a construction of clay and straw which was narrower at the top than at the bottom. The top needed covering to protect the unstable filling.

Sometimes architecture represents a chronological sequence. In the USA much history can be traced by studying buildings constructed at different stages of the country's growth. Examples of these are slave dwellings, southern mansions, skyscrapers and the Space Centre at Cape Canaveral.

Architecture can encapsulate a whole period – Georgian Bath, the New Lanark of Robert Owen or the London overspill towns like Harlow. Sometimes a whole story can be contained in a stately home such as Chatsworth House in Derbyshire.

Lever, J. and Harris, J. (1993) *Illustrated Dictionary of Architecture*. London: Faber.
English Heritage publish several pamphlets: *Principles of Repair* (1993) (XH11045); *Investigative Work on Historic Buildings* (1995) (XH10678); *Something Worth Keeping? Post-war Architecture in England* (1996) (XH20001); *Work on Historic Churches* (1994) (XH10724).

art. Certain artworks enhance and support the teaching of history. *Guernica*, by Picasso; the crowning of Napoleon by himself, in David's painting; and the Bayeux Tapestry are three such examples. The National Portrait Gallery is well worth a visit; it publishes excellent postcards and pamphlets. Posters often carry a punch to enliven any class, and the Imperial War Museum has a good selection. Kitchener's famous recruiting poster, 'Your Country Needs You', is one such example, and the later 1941 slogan from the Ministry of Information, 'Be Like Dad, Keep Mum', is comparably good. There are many others which would be a help to the history teacher.

English Heritage: *Art and the Historic Environment* (XP14002).

Asian history. This contains vast contrasts, partly because the continent is so large. There are four groups of countries: Central Asia, which includes China, Japan and the two Koreas; South East Asia, which includes Vietnam, Malaysia and Myanmar (Burma); Oceana, which includes Australia and New Zealand; and the Indian sub-continent. Nevertheless, the whole continent has major problems common to many of the countries: they are overpopulation, disease, poverty and unemployment. It has also been a turbulent continent politically, mainly due to conflict between those countries that have chosen communism as their political system and those who have not.

Prominent in all the civil wars has been the USA. The role of China, united under Mao Tse Tung, has also been powerful. Japan was able to recover quickly from the last war due to the policy of the USA to allow the Japanese to run their own government; they were also able to put money into their economy because they were not allowed to have any defence forces. Consequently, Japan has become the economic power-house of the Far East, while other countries, like Korea, were fighting civil wars to determine their futures, as was Vietnam. The USA has sought strenuously to stop the spread of communism, fearing it would affect adjacent countries – the 'domino' effect.

The wars in Korea and Vietnam, the development of China and the economic strength of Japan have all been portrayed so powerfully in films that it is relatively easy to engage students in the history of Asian countries. The difficulty for the teacher is to present a more even-handed presentation of the internal conflicts of the continent than the student will have seen in the cinema. Sometimes, reference to the old civilizations on the continent, like those of India and China, mentioning their landmark achievements in printing and gunpowder, for example, and their impact on Europe, arouse interest.

See separate entry on **imperialism and colonialism**.

assessment.   The process by which one person attempts to find out about the knowledge, attitudes or skills of another. In the USA the term 'evaluation' is preferred. There are particular skills that it is appropriate for the historian to possess, and thus be tested on, and these are considered under the heading **National Curriculum**.

Journal of Assessment in Education: Principle, Policy and Practice. Centre for Curriculum and Assessment Studies, Bristol University and the International Centre for Research on Assessment, London University Institute of Education.
SEAC (1990) A Source Book of Teacher Assessment.
SEAC (1991, 1992, 1993) School Assessment Folders.

Association of History and Computing.   Based at Queen Mary Westfield College (*see separate entry under **ICT***). It has a journal – the *Journal of the Association of History and Computing*. This is aimed at historians using computers for research and covers all aspects of computing applications, from quantitative methods to free-test analysis and image-processing, graphical presentation, project management, funding problems, communication and training. The journal is published by Edinburgh University Press, 22 George Street, Edinburgh EH8 9LF.

astrology.   The science of foretelling events by studying the positions and motions of heavenly bodies. Its history spans more than 2000 years and once covered everything from a general acceptance of stellar influences to precise definitions of stellar movements. Fifth-century Greece was where people began to study the stars for the first time. Then they added philosophy, geometry and rational thought. Plato made astrology respectable and by the second century the main lines of astrological practice had been laid down in the book *Tetrabiblos*. The book changed little when it was adopted by Islamic society, and the West, where it emerged in the twelfth century and again in the Renaissance. Queen Elizabeth I, for example, had her own Royal Adviser in Mystic Secrets, Dr John Dee (1527–1608), who was consulted on many subjects by the Queen, including the making of pure gold (which he failed to accomplish) and the date of her coronation. Eventually, in the sixteenth and seventeenth centuries, interest subsided but never completely disappeared.

'Astrology died, like an animal or plant left stranded by evolution. It was not killed' (Tester, 1990). Alexander de'Angeli, a Jesuit, in the *Praefalio Apologetica* of 1622, listed five objections to astrology: there were no clear basic principles; astrologists never completely answered criticisms; they were often just wrong; they had not always studied their own science enough; and they were often ignorant.

Tester, J. (1990) *A History of Western Astrology*. London, Boydell.
Thomas, K. (1971) *Religion and the Decline of Magic*. New York.

astronomy.   The study of the sun, moon, stars, planets and other celestial bodies. It is a science as old as time and has a history that is full of superstition, intellectual dispute and major scientific innovation. It has as much diversity within it as life itself, and this includes many areas that are still in need of investigation and research. Ancient astronomy was a known subject in Babylon where, amongst other things, they thought the earth was a disc of land surrounded by a moat of sea and surmounted by a solid firmament. It was indistinguishable at that time from **astrology**. The Egyptians, led by Ptolemy (AD 100–170), embraced many of the Babylonian ideas, including astrology, and introduced a 365-day year, which was then adopted by the Greeks. Pythagoras saw the Earth as a sphere and Aristotle conceived a finite, spherical universe centred on a stationary Earth. Little of significance changed until Nicolaus Copernicus (1473–1543) who, in his book *De Revolutionibus Orbium Coelestium*, published in 1543, claimed that the earth moved round the sun, and Johannes Kepler (1571–1630) proved that the planets moved around the sun in elliptical orbits. Galileo (1564–1642) further advanced astronomical science and undertook the first serious telescopic observation. **Newton** was the great pioneer in gravitational astronomy and in 1671, during his lifetime, the **Royal Society** was formed.

Modern astronomy was completely revolutionized by the introduction of a whole battery of innovations which included photography, radio waves, radio astronomy, artificial satellites, space exploration, probes, shuttles and space stations. Men have walked on the moon and probes have been sent to a whole range of planets including Mars. The first manned space flight was by the Russian Yuri Gagarin, closely followed by John Glenn who was the first American to orbit the Earth. The most recent invention has been the Hubble Space Telescope which has provided even more dramatic images of space. Thus the history of this complex but intriguing science has never ceased to develop. It has become the litmus paper of human endeavour.

Jones, B. (1991) *An Introduction to Practical Astronomy*. London: Apple.
Moore, P. (1993) *Guide to Stars and Planets*. London: Reed.

atlas.   It reveals lack of knowledge as bluntly as it provides information. It also provides a visual tool to 'unlocking the past' (Black, 1993). Today more information is being shown on maps than ever before. For example, Dockrill (1991) covers desertification, sea pollution, acid rain and tropical rainforest clearance in two maps. Spatial analysis by computer is in two dimensions, giving a fresh perspective. A diagram showing death in London in the cholera epidemic of 1849 is included in Hagget (1978). Popular cultural history is now included as well as 'elitist' culture. For example, the *Historical Atlas of Canada* has two maps devoted to the national broadcasting systems. The distribution of music is illustrated in the atlas of the United States and Canada Society.

Black, J. (1993) 'The historical atlas: a tool and its limitations'. *Teaching History, October.*
Dockrill, M. (1991) *Atlas of Twentieth Century World History*. London: Collins.
Haggets, C. and P. (1978) *Atlas of Disease Distributions: Analytic Approaches to Epidemiological Data*. Oxford: OUP.
Times (1997) *Historical Atlas*. London: Times Books.

Attainment Targets (ATs).   The knowledge, skills and understanding pupils of different abilities and maturities are expected to have acquired by the end of each Key Stage of the National Curriculum.

*See separate entry under **National Curriculum**.*

Australia.   Some of the issues and topics which are especially significant in this nation's rich history are:

Aboriginal land rights (*see separate entry under **indigenous people***);
Anzac (short for Australia and New Zealand Army Corps);
Australia Labour Party (including Whitlam, Hawke and Keating who were all PMs);
Australian Navy (which fought in both world wars);
Commonwealth of Australia (came into being on 1 January 1901: Australia is also a member of the British Commonwealth);
Exclusion Party;

Federation (the Australian Federation Convention first met in Adelaide in 1897, then in 1898; received royal assent 1900);
immigration;
Northern Territory;
Tasmania (separated from New South Wales in 1825 and is the largest island in the Australian Commonwealth);
transportation (chosen in 1786 as the destination for convicts);
Wakefield, Edward Gibbon (reformed land ownership in New South Wales; helped found South Australia);
White Australian Policy (restricted immigration into Australia);
wool (Australia is the world's leading producer).

See separate entry on **indigenous people**.

Clark, C. M. H. (1987) *A History of Australia*. Melbourne: Melbourne University Press.
Roberts, S. (1969) *History of Australian Land Settlement*. London: Cassell.

Australian Historical Association.   The AHA is based in Canberra, publishes a *Bulletin*, the *Electronic Journal of Australian and New Zealand History* and *H-ANZAU* – history news and newsgroups on line.

AHA Secretariat, Department of History, Research School of Social Science, Australian National University, Canberra ACT 0200, Australia; e-mail: nether@cyllene.usa.edu.au; website: http://www/arts.uwa.edu.au/aha/index.html

B

baccalauréat.   The French school-leaving examination, taken at 18 or 19 years of age. The International Baccalaureate is a post-16 examination which is tested by examination in six contrasted subjects: three main, which take two years; and three subsidiary, which take one year. The history syllabus is a World History one with several options (*see separate entry on **world history***). It is an accepted university-entry qualification.

French Embassy Cultural Department, 23 Cromwell Road, London SW7 2EL.

International Baccalauréate Organization, 1218 Grand-Saconnex, Geneva (main office); 130 Route de Morillous 15, Geneva. Tel: 0041 22791 0274.

Peterson House, Fortram Road, St Mellons, Cardiff CS3 0LT (British office).

balance of power.   A concept which seeks to obtain peace by ensuring that no nation is unduly preponderant. The term was first used in the Treaty of Utrecht 1713, which had ended the War of the Spanish Succession. This was a peace between Britain and France on the one hand and Spain on the other. It was designed to 'contain' French ambitions for the immediate future, but when France became militant during the French Revolutionary Wars the balance of power collapsed. As the nineteenth century unfolded and nationalism developed, the balance of power was sacrificed. The territorial and military successes of Napoleon, Cavour and Bismarck not only strengthened the power of individual countries but also encouraged those countries to seek further territory. The country which seriously challenged any possibility of returning to an eighteenth-century balance of power was Britain, through the Empire. At one point, at the end of the nineteenth century, the British Empire covered a fifth of the world's land mass and was the largest empire the world has seen. Any balance of power was impossible in such a context.

The Cold War, following the 1945 peace, was based on tension between the USSR and the USA – a modern version of the balance of power. Behind the two powerful nations ranged the communist Eastern European Warsaw Pact (led by the USSR) on the one hand, and the NATO (1949) capitalist democracies on the other. Behind these two blocs was what Churchill, in a speech at Fulton, Missouri, in March 1946, described as an Iron Curtain across Europe. Interestingly, this ideological division broke up with the destruction of the Berlin Wall which had become the physical symbol of it.

Beloff, M. (1968) *The Balance of Power.* London: Allen and Unwin.
Sheehan, M. (1995) *The Balance of Power: History and Theory.* London: Routledge.

Bath Museum of Costume.   Housed in Bath's eighteenth-century Assembly Rooms it is one of the most extensive collections of its kind. There are displays of 200 dressed figures and examples of changing styles from the late sixteenth century to the present day. The Museum also contains a fashion research centre, a library of books on the history of dress from the medieval period to the present day, exhibition catalogues from museums around the world and a number of shop catalogues. There are photographic records, records of the couture houses, and knitting and embroidery patterns. Of special interest for school pupils is the 'Study Collection' which can be used by special arrangement and is a 'handling collection of fashionable dress, accessories and small number of flat textiles dating from the late eighteenth century to the present day'. The museum suggests that students of GCSE level upwards look at objects in the Study Collection. The Study Collection seats up to eight students and there is a charge of £2 per head, payable on arrival. Booking reservations should be made to: The Fashion Research Centre, 4 The Circus, Bath BA1 2EW. It is also wise to book a place in the library by telephoning 01225 477754 in advance, as space is limited.

Bath Museum of Costume, Assembly Rooms, Bennett Street, Bath. Tel: 01225 477789; fax: 01225 4447989; e-mail: costume@bath-nes.gov.uk; website: www.museum of costume.co.uk

Bayeux Tapestry.   Worthy of special mention because it is the oldest surviving wall-hanging. It was probably commissioned in 1077 by Odo of Bayeux for the dedication of his rebuilt cathedral, but the precise date and origin are disputed. It describes and is a factual basis for, a long period of important Norman history. It clearly illustrates clothes, weapons and lifestyle of the period. It is not the only source of such information because it is matched by some documents, but, nevertheless, it is useful. It is an embroidered strip of linen 68 metres long and half a metre wide. It is housed in atmospherically controlled showcases in a museum in Bayeux.

Bernstein, D. J. (1986) *The Mystery of the Bayeux Tapestry.* London: Weidenfeld & Nicholson.
Maclagan, Eric (1943) *The Bayeux.* London: King Penguin.
Stenton, F. (1965) *Bayeux Tapestry: A Comprehensive Survey.* London: Phaidon.

Website: the Bayeux Tapestry http://flight of the dragon.com/kyl/ clipart/bayeux tapestry

Bede (c. 672/3–735). Often described as the Father of English History because he wrote *The Ecclesiastical History of the English Church and People.* He completed this in about AD 731. It was written in Latin and translated by Alfred in the ninth century. He gathered material from several sources and had a colleague researching for him in the papal archives. It is still one of the most accurate accounts of the history of England from the time of the Roman occupation until the eighth century. It is accurate, readable and remarkably comprehensive.

Bede was born in Wearmouth in about AD 672 and entered a local monastery at the age of 7. He was transferred to a new foundation at Jarrow where he spent the rest of his life and wrote 40 books on the Bible, biographies of saints, primers on Latin and astronomy and a technical work of calculations to determine the date of Easter. The last was prompted by the decision of the Synod of Whitby in AD 664 that the English Church should adopt the Roman method of determining the date of the feast. Bede died on the eve of Ascension Day in AD 735, and is buried in Durham Cathedral.

The translation of his *History* is readily available and his literary style is easy to read. To analyse passages of the text with a group of students is to get a glimpse of an era that is not easy to obtain in other ways except, possibly, through a few well-preserved buildings. Another interesting approach, in addition to reading selective passages, is to encourage some detective work by tracing his original sources, like Tacitus (AD 55–120) and the life of his father-in-law Agricola, and to compare these other early histories with the Bede account. It is another piece of helpful detective work to 'spot' his references to the claim that the English were a single people – the first time it had been so expressed.

Bede (1955) *A History of the English Church and People* (trans. Leo Sherley-Price). Harmondsworth: Penguin.

bias and prejudice. These are not the same, but are allied enough to justify being considered together. Bias is an unfair influence; prejudice is an unreasonable dislike or a one-sided view. Hitler had an unreasonable dislike of the Jews. Historians of the Trades Union Congress have a bias in favour of the Tolpuddle Martyrs, even though the Martyrs broke the law quite deliberately. The Monmouth Rebellion was a treasonable revolt against the King and yet some publicity surrounding the insurrection is prejudiced in favour of the rebels. One man's bias is another man's anathema, so writing about bias and prejudice will always receive a mixed reception.

Edmund Burke (1729–97) was clear that society depended on what he called prejudice, that is on instinctive feelings of love and loyalty. This, plus his rejection of the central place revolutionary thinkers had given to reason, led to his critique of natural law and natural rights. He believed in 'the beautiful order of society bonded by loyalties and prejudice'. William Hazlitt, in 'On Prejudice' (1830), saw the matter with deceptive simplicity: 'Without the aid of prejudice and custom, I should not be able to find my way across the room.'

Moss, P. (1976) *Prejudice and Discrimination*. London: Harrap.

Bible in English. The Bible contains the Scriptures of the Old and New Testament which are really a collection of several books and which have been translated into over 1000 languages. Apart from a few paraphrases, attributed to Caedmon, and the translation by Bede of part of the Gospel of St John, the earliest attempts at translation into English are the ninth- and tenth-century versions of the Psalms and the tenth-century versions of the Gospels. The first translation from Latin into English was by Nicholas of Hereford and John Purvey, about 1390. It is doubtful if much of this was by John Wyclif, as is often claimed. The next significant translation was by William Tyndale in the 1520s, which was revised by Miles Coverdale in 1535. The Authorized Version, the King James Bible, was published in 1611 and the Revised Version in 1881–5. The New English Bible was published in 1961 (New Testament) and 1970 (Old Testament) and was the result of research by a group of biblical scholars. The Revised English Bible was published with the full support of the Roman Catholic Church in 1989.

Chronology is an essential part of our understanding of the Bible whether it is seen as a spiritual guide, an historical library or both. It is intrinsic to the cultural inheritance of England and of young people, whether they are Christians or not.

The reading of the Bible would be an innovation and useful exercise for the majority of schoolchildren. A compendium of different translations would enable students to make their own comparisons and reach their own conclusions about which one they prefer.

'No book has had a more profound and lasting influence on the religious life, the history, the culture, the institutions and the language of the English-speaking people throughout the world than has the King James Bible' (P. D. James in the *Sunday Times Culture* Supplement, 30 May 1999).

Modern versions of the Bible include: the Good News Bible (1976); the Jerusalem Bible (1966); the Knox translation (1955); the Moffatt translation (1934); the New English Bible (Old and New Testaments) (1970) (OUP and CUP); and The Revised Standard (1993).

Keller, Werner (1956) (trans. William Neil) *The Bible as History.* London: Hodder and Stoughton.

The New Testament in Four Versions (1967). London: Collins.

biography and autobiography.   Biography is the written life of a person and is intrinsic to the study of history. Nevertheless, it is often marginalized by teachers. Biography has several functions for the teacher. It can bring a 'human' quality to an otherwise dry lesson; it is sometimes the essence of a subject, as in the political struggle between Stalin and Trotsky; it is sometimes the only way of explaining how a set of circumstances occurred, as in the rise to power of Hitler; it often provides an arresting introduction, as with the fact that Martin Luther had stomach ulcers as he led opposition to the teachings of the Catholic Church; it can often illuminate the times in which a particular person lived, as in the life of Charles Dickens. So it is always interesting and usually preferable to use a biographical approach. An often unrecognized by-product is that students become drawn to reading on their own account because biographies make compulsive reading. There are classic biographies, such as Elizabeth Gaskell's *Life of Charlotte Bronte*, or J. S. Mill's autobiography.

The *Dictionary of National Biography* is a valuable resource and is found in most large libraries. It is comprehensive and is being constantly updated. There is also a three-volume *Concise Dictionary of National Biography*, published by the Oxford University Press in 1992 and by Softback Review in 1994, which is also valuable for teaching.

Swindles, J. (ed.) (1995) *The Uses of Autobiography.* London: Taylor and Francis.

Black Power movement in the USA.   The movement became especially active in the 1960s and took a strident approach to civil rights. At that time there were still separate lavatories for black and white men and women in many parts of the States, and seating in buses was often segregated. It was worst in the south. Leaders such as Stokeley Carmichael proposed that black Americans should establish their own power bases independent of white people, and in 1966 the Student Non-Violent Co-ordinating Committee (SNCC) was formed. The Black Muslim movement advocated Islam as the salvation for blacks, while at the same time the Black Panthers advocated violence. There were riots in many American cities, but these tended to die out as black organizations co-operated with white groups against the Vietnam War. The Black Muslim movement eventually lost its drive and thrust due to serious divisions between those who advocated peaceful means and those who wanted to adopt more violent methods of ending racial integration.

Carmichael, S. (1969) *Black Power: The Politics of Liberation in America.* Harmondsworth: Penguin.

British Library. A copyright library, which means it should contain every book published in this country. It is one of five such copyright libraries, the others being the National Library of Wales in Aberystwyth, the National Library of Scotland in Edinburgh, the Bodleian Library in Oxford, the Cambridge University Library and the Library of Trinity College, Dublin.

Situated in Euston Road, London, it is a custom-made library with high-quality facilities and services. It also includes exhibition space. The material is constantly changing and the library has a range of facilities to engage students of any age. There is also a helpful education section.

British Library, 96 Euston Road, London NW1 2DB, UK. Tel: 0207 412 7111; fax: 0207 412 7268.

British Museum. The Museum was instituted in 1759, and the circular Reading Room in 1852–7. It houses many great collections which are still being augmented with gifts from all over the world. It contains shops and a restaurant and conducts guided tours. In addition, exhibitions of international importance are held, and there is a programme of lectures throughout the year. The Museum also produces valuable CD-ROMs of its collections. These cover study units in National Curriculum History; for example *The Making of the UK Medieval Realms.*

British Museum, Great Russell Street, London WC1B 3DG, UK. Tel: 0207 636 1555; fax: 0207 323 8118; e-mail: pr-bm@mailbox. ulcc.ac.uk

Bruner. Jerome Bruner (b.1915) established the Center for Cognitive Studies at Harvard in 1960. He concentrated on developing language skills, believing they were central to thought development. He did not agree with Piaget that children passed through different stages of thinking development but thought instead that children used different types of thinking according to the problem they had to solve or the situation in which they found themselves. His books include: *The Process of Education* (1960) and *Child's Talk: Learning to Use Language* (1983).

C

Calvin. John Calvin (1509–64) was born in Noyon, France, the twelfth son of a prosperous Catholic family. He was educated first in Noyon, then in Paris, Orleans and Bourges. In 1533 he was converted to the Reformed religion, and in 1536 published the *Institutes of Religion*, which represents the heart of his theology: 'Il n'y a pas de theologia perennis, mais uniquement des tentatives provisoires destinées a nourrir on à expliciter la vie actuelle de la communauté chrétienne.'

Seven years later followed the *Ecclesiastical Ordinances* (1541) which set out a range of specific principles enshrined in a form of church government. Calvin was by then representing a clear belief in predestination – God's fore-ordaining of what will come to pass – and with it the minimizing of the freedom of the human will. He fully justified legitimate resistance to ungodly authority. He became the architect of Genevan government, which was organized strictly according to the rules, doctrine and organization of his Christian Community outlined in the *Institutes*: moral behaviour according to strict principles was rigidly enforced and deviants were punished. The influence of Calvin's theological ideas had a profound influence on sixteenth- and seventeenth-century Puritanism in parts of Europe, especially Switzerland, England and North America.

A worthwhile student exercise would be to discuss with a local United Reformed church in England or a Presbyterian church in the USA the nature of their organization and theology and any possible comparisons with Calvin's ideas.

'New Presbyter is but old Priest writ large,' wrote John Milton on the forcers of conscience. The word 'forcer' means one who forces.

Parkes, T. H. L. (1995) *Calvin: An Introduction to his Thought*. London: Chapman.
Wendel, F. (1997) *Calvin*. Grand Rapids Michigan, USA: Baker Books.

Canada.   Canadian history is colourful, dynamic and has at least three dimensions which need to be appreciated. One is its attitude towards independence which, though distinctive, is not unique and bears interesting comparison with the USA and Australia. Another is the cultural nature of the country which comes partly from being bilingual but also from its geographical location on the North American continent. The third is the powerful effect of having the USA as a neighbour. To appreciate fully the effect of these different historical dimensions requires an understanding of three aspects of Canadian history: its relations with Britain, its relations with the USA and the role of the French rather than the French Government. All of these helped to shape the Canadian nation and in many ways they still do.

The challenge in teaching the history of this country is to understand fully the ways in which Canada looks outwards – to the USA; to Europe, as a member of NATO, in particular to Britain and France; and to Central America in, for example, the trade agreement with Mexico. It is challenging for every other country that Canada has sought an international role almost from the moment it achieved Dominion Status, which was effectively independence. Canadians live with such openness because it is part of their inheritance but other countries would do well to observe the ease with which they shoulder such a national identity. The history of Canada contains major events such as the Durham Report and the Monroe Doctrine, but these belong to a country which embraces the policy of *maître chez nous*.

Franks, C. E. S. (1987) *The Parliament of Canada*. London: University of Toronto Press.
Lanclot, G. (1964) *A History of Canada*. Toronto: Clarke Irwin.
Commonwealth Institute, Canada (1968): *Selected Reading List*. London: Commonwealth Institute.

Canadian Catholic Historical Association.   A national society, founded in 1933, for the promotion of and interest in the history of the Canadian Catholic Church. It encourages research and the presentation and understanding of sites, buildings, documents and 'heirlooms of the past'. It has printed and distributed Historical Studies since 1964, which include an annual bibliography of church history. It also publishes a twice-yearly bulletin.

115 Yonge Street, Toronto, ON, M4T1W2. Tel: (416) 934 0606; fax: (416) 934 3444; website: http://www.umanitoba.ca/colleges/stpauls/ccha/index2.htwl

Canadian Historical Association.   An internationally recognized bilingual association founded in 1922. It was incorporated in 1970. Members include professional historians employed in universities, colleges, high schools and governments, as well as institutions and members of the general public with interests in history and heritage preservation. It organizes conferences, publishes a bilingual catalogue and several journals.

Department of History, York University, 4700 Keele Street, North York, Ontario, M3J1P3. E-mail: swall@yorku.ca; website: wysiwyg:/ /fl.80/http://www.homestead.com/chagrad/English Home – ns4.html

cartoons.   Satirical drawings which often deal with politics. They are useful because they encapsulate a whole issue or incident, give insight into a contemporary situation, are easily available and are usually funny. A joke drawing often becomes a 'memory peg' and is timeless. *Punch* is one of the most popular sources, and cartoons from old copies of this magazine are used regularly as the basis for examination questions. Cartoon questions in past papers are therefore permanently useful for current internal exams or classwork. Indeed, the kind of exam questions which are based upon a cartoon are a valuable method of introducing a class to documentary analysis.

Coven, A. (1983) *Pick of Punch*. London: Hutchinson.
Seymour-Ure, Colin and Ottoway, Liz (1990) 'Newspaper Cartoons'. *MHR*, **1**(3) February, 26–7.
Stanyon, Anne (1993) 'Cartoons as a Historical Source'. *MHR*, **3**(3), April.

castles.   Fortified dwellings that were fully developed in England by the Normans and often used to control or dominate an area. Early castles were based on a motte-and-bailey design, a wooden stockade on top of a mound or hill. But these early buildings were often replaced by stone on the same site. Some of the most important castles of the thirteenth century were built in the reign of Edward I in Wales. Outside Britain there are even more impressive castles, such as the Chateau Gaillard in Normandy or the Krak des Chevaliers in Syria. Eventually, however, these heavily fortified castles in England and Europe were replaced by unfortified manor houses as society became less warlike and more settled. During the Middle Ages castles were often schools for knights and young aristocratic men who would be sent away to friends of their fathers to learn the essential responsibilities and art of being a knight.

'For a man's house is his castle, and a man's home is his safest refuge' (Sir Edward Coke (1552–1634) *The Third Part of the Institutes of the Laws of England* (1628), ch. 73).

English Heritage has a range of videos and booklets for specific sites; for example, Scarborough Castle (01723 372451), which has a free audio tour, souvenir guidebook and children's activity sheet.

See separate entry under **heritage**.

cathedrals. The principal seat of a diocesan bishop. Cathedrals were either secular or monastic in foundation, and by the time of the Norman Conquest were founded mainly in centres of population. They became rich and famous and were always connected with saints; sometimes local saints with a cult following, such as St Alban. They also developed exciting architectural styles; Salisbury, Durham, Lincoln, Canterbury and York are good examples.

When the monasteries were dissolved five new dioceses were created: Chester, Gloucester, Peterborough, Oxford and Bristol. During the seventeenth and eighteenth centuries many cathedrals suffered from neglect or Civil War vandalism and, apart from the building of St Paul's in London, there was little new building until the nineteenth century; nineteen new dioceses were created between 1836 and 1945. Sir Basil Spence's rebuilding of Coventry Cathedral became a symbol of postwar reconstruction and peace.

The re-establishment of the Roman Catholic hierarchy in England has led to new cathedrals being built in a variety of styles, from the neo-Byzantine style of Westminster Cathedral to the ultra-modern Liverpool and Bristol.

Always a rich treasury of music, documents, stained glass, brass-rubbing centres and precious artefacts, cathedrals are important to visit for their history, quite apart from their spiritual significance. It is satisfying that those foundations which were once places of learning, through their schools, colleges and clerical academies, have become important centres again through the visits of students of all kinds and ages. In very different ways these spiritual and intellectual centres have remained the precious repositories they have always been. All of them, ancient and modern, Anglican and Roman Catholic, repay study and first-hand familiarity.

> I think that cars today are almost the exact equivalent of the great Gothic Cathedrals: I mean the supreme creation of an era, conceived with passion by unknown artists, and consumed in image if not in usage by a whole population which appropriates them a purely magical effect. (Barthes, R. (1915–80) *Mythologies 'La Nouvelle Citroen'* (1957))

Courtenay, Lynn T. (ed.) (1997) *The Engineering of Medieval Cathedrals*. Aldershot: Ashgate.
Meyer, P. (1950) *English Cathedrals*. London: Thames and Hudson.

See separate entry under **heritage**.

celibate. One who has taken solemn vows not to marry and who has chosen to dedicate his or her life to God and the Church. History throughout the world has been influenced deeply by those who have taken this decision. In Christianity, monks and nuns and many priests have taken the vow of celibacy so that they could devote their lives to prayer, worship or evangelism.

Monasteries belong to various orders, such as the Benedictines, who follow the Rule of St Benedict, or the Eastern Orthodox who follow the Rule of St Basil. The cultural contribution of these establishments has been considerable and has included running schools, libraries, medical centres and places of refuge for the sick, the persecuted or those who have required spiritual refreshment. The three vows which most Christian religious take are poverty, chastity and obedience.

Buddhists also have their own monastic order called the *sangha* with its own code of discipline. Zen Buddhists have a comparable order.

It is important that students realize that there are people in the world who are moved by spiritual and not material considerations and who look to a life beyond this one. But it is also important to realize that religious (the collective noun for monks and nuns), have made a major contribution to the material conditions of people's lives. The contribution they have made in the arts – in architecture, sculpture, painting, calligraphy, weaving and needlework – has been great, both in quality and influence.

Central Office of Information (COI). A valuable source of recent history. It produces booklets, leaflets, films, radio and television material, exhibitions and other visual material.

Hercules House, Hercules Road, London SE1 7DU. Tel: 0207 928 2345; fax: 0207 928 5037; website: www.coi.gov.uk

Certificate of Achievement. Introduced in 1998 as a qualification for school leavers who would otherwise leave school without qualifications in history or any other subject. GCSE criteria do not apply to CoAs, which are awarded at three levels comparable to levels 1, 2 and 3 of the National Curriculum.

Certificate of Secondary Education. Introduced in 1965 for school leavers for whom the GCSE Ordinary Level was considered to be too hard. It was abolished in 1988 at the same time as the GCE Ordinary Level, and both the CSE and the GCE were replaced by the GCSE.

*See separate entry under **National Curriculum**.*

Charlemagne Charles the First, The Great. Charlemagne (*c.*742–814) was one of the most distinguished people of the Middle Ages. He was the son of Pepin III and grandson of Charles Martel. He was King of the Franks and set about imposing his rule. He began a campaign in 772 against the Saxons, then against the Avars, Bavaria and Lombardy, to restore the papal lands to the papacy. On

Christmas Day 800 he was crowned Emperor of the West by Pope Leo III. His capital city was Aachen and it became an important centre of learning in western Christendom attracting scholars like Alcuin (c. 737–804), who became a leading adviser on intellectual and educational matters. Schools were founded throughout Europe and the revival of scholarship, which began during Charlemagne's reign, is sometimes call the Carolingian Renaissance. 'Charlesmagne a ouvert les portes de l'avenir. Et pour cela seul il meriterait le nom de Grand' (*Librarie Larousse Canada*, 1973). 'This agglomeration which was called and still calls itself the Holy Roman Empire was neither holy, not Roman, nor an Empire in any way' (Voltaire, *Essai sur le moeurs et l'esprit des nations, lxx*).

Chata project.   Funded by the Economic and Social Research Council (ESRC) as part of their research programme 'Innovation and Change in Education: The Quality of Teaching and Learning'. Peter Lee and Alanic Dickinson are co-directors of the project and Rosalyn Ashby is the Project Officer.

The main aims are to increase understanding of the

> progression of childrens' second-order concepts of evidence and explanation in history (phase I), to develop characterizations of teaching approaches specific to history (phase II), and to explore relationships between teaching strategies and curriculum contexts on the one hand and childrens' understanding of second-order historical concepts on the other (phase III). Part of its potential importance to education is in extending knowledge and understanding of progression in history, grounding history teaching objectives in empirical evidence of how childrens' ideas develop between the ages of seven and fourteen. (Lee *et al.*, 1996, p. 6)

Lee, P., Dickinson, A. and Ashby, R. (1996) 'Project Chata: Concepts of History and Teaching Approaches at Key Stages 2 and 3', *TH*, 82, January, 6–11.

children.   Chimney-sweeps and child slaves in factories and mines are familiar areas to make contrasts with present-day society. There are also stories about elementary education in schools which appal by their rigidity and discipline. But less publicized are the tales of misbehaviour, such as the wild boys of Rugby School who wandered around the countryside of Warwickshire in the nineteenth century uncontrolled. For most children, especially girls, most education took place in the home and this led to a perpetuation of good and bad habits. If the father was a craftsman he would pass on his precious and considerable skills. If the parent was incapable or lazy the results were not always so good.

For some, in rural areas particularly, accommodation was provided in dormitory style for both young children and adolescents who were put to work on the land, either under the direction of the farmer or his wife. Aristocratic boys would be sent away to another manor house where they would be taught by a friend of the family how to be gentlemen. If they went to one of the Inns of Court, or to Oxford or Cambridge, they would be accompanied by a peasant boy from the village who would act as servant or page. Often the servant graduated from the college with equal distinction. Girls, by contrast, stayed at home and had few chances to improve themselves through formal education, until the twentieth century. Childhood was, for many, a sad time.

Two items of royal history are worth particular mention: one is that Queen Victoria was only eighteen when she ascended the throne (her father had died when she was eight months old); the other is the probable murder of the two princes in the Tower. Edward V (1470–83) was King of England between April and June 1483 and was the eldest surviving son of Edward IV. His Protector, Richard Duke of Gloucester, imprisoned the young prince, with his younger brother Richard, in the Tower of London because he claimed they were illegitimate and that he, Richard, was the rightful heir to the throne. Richard proclaimed himself King by Parliament and the princes were not heard of again. They were probably murdered, but this has never been proved.

In the eighteenth century the ideas of pioneer philosophers like Jean Jacques Rousseau, Johann Pestalozzi and Friedrich Froebel helped, slowly, to improve the education of children. Their ideas were further enhanced in the twentieth century by Maria Montessori, Jean Piaget and Susan Isaacs.

Christianity. The world's most popular religion with over 1000 million followers. It is divided into several sects, the largest being the Roman Catholic Church. All Christians believe in the teachings of Jesus Christ and that he was born, lived, was crucified and rose again in the Holy Land, most of which is now the state of Israel. He chose twelve disciples who carried forward his message contained in the New Testament, and now the beliefs and teachings of Christ have spread throughout the world. In 1054 there was a split between the western church – the Roman Catholic Church – and the Eastern Church, which became known as Orthodox. Another split occurred in the early sixteenth century when Martin Luther attacked the authority of the Pope and many of the practices of the church (*see separate entry under **Luther***). He was soon joined by John **Calvin** and others who broke away. This Protestant separation was soon answered by the Catholic Counter-Reformation but separate from both of these, and yet associated with them, was the breaking away of the Church of England under Henry VIII, followed by its partial reconciliation under his daughter, Elizabeth I. She sought to create an 'umbrella' national church in which Protestant and Catholic could worship together. Some Christians would not worship with any of the established churches and either formed their own, e.g. the Methodists, or set sail to America (the Pilgrim Fathers). As Christianity spread and carried the Gospel message, it also carried with it many divisions caused by differing interpretations of the Scriptures by the various factions and sects within it.

Christianity has three aspects which justify consideration by all students, whether they are Christian or not. The first is that it contains a set of spiritual beliefs which many people hold to be precious. There are also large numbers who live by similar beliefs but who are not Christians. The second aspect worthy of our attention is the cultural inheritance of Christianity. This includes buildings, music, art, colour, the use of language and the fact that Christian worship and practice has motivated large numbers of individuals and sometimes whole civilizations. Thirdly, the Christian Church has created a legal framework for general administration which has had a permanent effect upon society in general. Justinian's *Codex, Digest and Institutes* came with Christianity, were designed for a Christian society and now form the basis of most legal systems.

See separate entries under the **Bible**, *the* **Reformation**, **Luther** *and* **Calvin**.

Edwards, D. L. (1998) *A Concise History of English Christianity.* London: Fount.
Fernandez-Amesto, F. and Wilson, D. (1996) *Christianity and the World 1500–2000.* London: Bantam.

chronology.   A science which arranges historical dates and periods in order. In the preface to his *Brief Survey of History*, George Townsend Warner wrote:

> It has sometimes been taken for granted that the right method of teaching history is to lay down a preliminary groundwork of facts and dates and miscellaneous scraps of important information, before making an attempt to awaken interest in the connection of historical events by the process of reasoning. The principle is somewhat akin to the mode of teaching languages by grinding over grammar and accidence; it is at any rate time-honoured.

Cosmo Landesman, interviewing Antony Beevor, in the *Sunday Times* (20 June 1999) puts a very different viewpoint:

> The teaching of history is being done very badly – all this touchy-feely empathy stuff gives nobody a real idea of how things really were. Let me give you an example. I have a friend who teaches history to medical students. They know who Queen Victoria was, but have no idea which century she lived in. They know Napoleon was a general, but have no idea what is meant by the Napoleonic era. Today few students have any idea what came before or after what.

Tim Chapman writes, in an article entitled 'Teaching chronology through timelines' (*TH*, **73**, October 1993, 25–6):

Timelines are just one tool useful for developing chronology, both for single studies of particular changes but also for comparative work. They allow pupils to work with greater independence and a wider vocabulary. They are useful as introductions to and conclusions of topics, and above all, they help to explain to pupils the concept of time. Chronology is a key element in the history syllabus of the National Curriculum.

See separate entry on time and on **National Curriculum.**

Beevor, A. (1998) *Stalingrad.* London: Viking.
Ibid. (1996) *Journal of Curriculum Studies,* **28**(5), Sept/Oct, 531–76.
Madeley, H. M. (1948) *Time Charts.* London: HA Pamphlet 50.
Warner, G. T. (1900) *Brief Survey of History.* London: Blackie.

churches and chapels. These form the evidence of Christianity in Britain. They are icons built for spiritual and religious purposes. They then *become* spiritual and religious in their own right. The insides of churches and chapels usually contain a variety of artefacts that tell the story of the ways in which people worshipped in those buildings. Churches and chapels are evidence of the way people lived and expressed their religious convictions.

A useful source of information about Anglican churches can be obtained from the nearest cathedral.

The National Association of Decorative and Fine Arts Societies runs a system of recording the contents of churches. Not only is their survey work very detailed, it is also accurate. They will be able to provide information on the nearest branch which is certain to be within twenty miles of even the most remote location. Their address is: Nadfas House, 6 Guilford Street, London WC1N 1DT. Tel: 0207 430 0730.

See separate entry on **cathedrals.**

English Heritage have a leaflet on *Churches and Chapels* (XH10679).
Needham, A. (1944) *How to Study an Old Church.* London: Batsford.

citizenship. This is a contentious issue; it refers to the rights, responsibilities and political position and role of the citizen in a democratic society. Professor Bernard Crick, in his *Report on the Teaching of Citizenship and Democracy in Schools* (1997), claims that

> A main aim for the whole community should be to find or restore a sense of common citizenship that is secure enough to find a place for the plurality of nations, cultures and ethnic identifications and religions long found in the United Kingdom. (quoted in the *Guardian,* May 1999)

This bold and assertive aspiration has serious implications, in a democratic society, for the direct and indirect teaching of citizenship, which as always rested, in whole or in part, on the shoulders of the history teacher.

See separate entry on **National Curriculum**.

Centre for Citizenship Studies in Education (1994) 'Citizenship in primary schools' and 'Citizenship and values education in primary schools'. Two papers published by the Centre, based at Queens Building, Barrack Road, Nottingham NN2 6AF.

Edward, J. and Fogelman, K. (eds) (1993) *Developing Citizenship in the Curriculum*. London: David Fulton.

Edwards, J. and Trott, C. (1995) 'Education for citizenship for Key Stages 1 and 2'. *Curriculum Journal*, **6**(3), Autumn. *TH*, 78.

Encouraging Citizenship (1990). Report of the Speaker's Commission on Citizenship. London: HMSO.

Hahn, C. L. (1999) 'Citizenship Education'. *Oxford Review of Education*, **12**(1).

Holliday, J. (1999) 'Political liberalism and citizenship education'. *British Journal of Educational Studies*, **47**.

NCC (1990) 'Education for Citizenship'. *Curriculum Guidelines*, **8**. York: National Curriculum Council.

Walters, T. (1993) 'Good citizens in the making'. *Nursery World*, September.

classroom aids, apparatus and materials.   These are helpful but few teachers use all that is available. Some of the more familiar items, including some that are no longer fashionable, are: blackboards, chalk boards, white boards, magnet boards, flipcharts; charts, friezes, pictures; worksheets; thermal copiers, photocopiers, duplicators, stencils; overhead projectors, episcopes, epidiascopes; television, videos, interactive videos, CD-ROMs, video cameras; **film**, film loops, **slides**, **film strips**; **photographs**, cameras, digital cameras in association with computers; computers, micro-computers (*see separate entry on* **information and communications technology**); sound recordings, **radio**; classroom displays of pupils' work, story boards.

Leclerc, M. (1985) *Classroom Aids, Apparatus and Materials*. Stafford: National Association for Remedial Education.

Warren, A., Brunner, D., Maier, P. and Barnett, L. (1998) *Technology in Teaching and Learning*. London: Kogan Page.

cognitive domain.   The area of learning involved in the acquisition of information, concepts and principles. Bloom created a taxonomy of cognitive objectives.

See separate entries on **affective learning** *and on* **Bruner**.

Bloom, B. (1956) *Taxonomy of Educational Objectives*. London: Longmans.

comics.   Periodicals composed mainly of pictures with an accompanying narrative. It is useful for any teacher to read a few. They can be an effective means of communication between teacher and pupil.

In France, lurid youth publications, *la bande dessinée*, abound, and in Japan the whole of male society, not just young people, seems drawn to comics. In Germany attitudes to history are being changed by instructive comic-books. For example, the CD-ROM 'So Go to the Other Side', covers German history in 56 pages and tells of: two related families from the east and the west, the exodus from Central Europe, German prisoners of war in Siberia, reconstruction in East and West Germany, the building of the Berlin Wall, the influence of the Stasi secret police, Red Army terrorism and the arson attacks on neo-Nazi gangs in the nineties. The soap-box hero is a young, handsome priest, and his attractiveness in the comic results in an important chunk of modern German history being more easily learned.

Roger Boyes, in an article in *The Times* (31 July 1999) called 'A funny way to learn history', wrote: 'One of the dangers is that though it [the comic] may bring history and literature closer to the young, it can also dull their reaction to tragedy.' Comics thrive on repetition, and this can be a strength or a weakness, especially when the characterization is always the same. This echoes Boyes's point about tragedy in that death may appear to be commonplace.

Scott Macleod wrote, in his book *Understanding Comics* (London, Pond Press, 1994), that 'There are no limits to the possibilities opened up by the comic book.'

communism. A social, economic and political ideology which gives power to the community. It is often thought to have originated either in Greece, in early Christianity or in Renaissance humanism. However, Marx, Lenin and Stalin, and their contemporaries, currently predominate the thinking on the subject. Of even greater importance is the interest which is still being shown towards the ideology by students.

In Soviet Russia, Lenin (1870–1924) advocated state control of all aspects of society. This involved controlling the organs of state and planning the central ownership of property. It subsequently spread all over the world; to China under Mao, to Cuba under Castro, to Vietnam under Ho Chi Min and to most countries of Eastern Europe after the 1939–45 War. As a political philosophy it was criticized for economic inefficiency, lack of political democracy and the denial of basic freedoms, and so, gradually, the 'dictatorship of the proletariat' found less and less support. Communist governments were overthrown and the climax came with the collapse of the Soviet Union in 1991.

A teaching context in which to understand the communist point of view is to compare political comment in different newspapers on an important question of the day. The range of papers would, of course, include the communist *Morning Star*. This will enable students to form their own opinions about the opinions expressed. Two earlier writers are worth a mention: Leon Trotsky:

> There is a limit to the application of democratic methods. You can inquire of all the passengers as to what type of car they like to ride in, but it is impossible to question them as to whether to apply the brakes when the train is at full speed and accident threatens. (*History of the Russian Revolution*, Part III, ch. 6);

and the Sheffield poet Ebenezer Elliot:

> What is a communist? One who hath yearnings
>   For equal division of unequal earnings. 'Epigrams' (1850)

See separate entries on **Hegel**, **Marx**, **Stalinism** *and* **Leninism**, *and* **North Atlantic Treaty Organization** *(which includes the Cold War).*

compact disc-read only memory.   CD-ROMs work like a music CD but can contain text, pictures and sound. More and more CD-ROMs are appearing which are clear and easy to use. The contents page gives a set of options displayed graphically. The index is shown as an option on part of the page design but students often need guidance in learning how to choose from what is available so that they discover how to look things up, how to choose what is best to select and how to structure the information obtained. The fact that students often look as though they are masters of the machine, which they often are, does not mean that they have the capacity to select material wisely. The reference roms which are very flexible, and the computerized reference book will find so many related cards and pages that it can be bewildering. Particular skills are required to ask the right question, knowing exactly how to look things up, being able to use the resources on offer and fitting all this information into a structure that is understood. Prices vary greatly. The *Daily Mail Centenary* costs £30, *Changing Times* costs £99 and the *Dictionary of National Biography*, with 40,000 entries in the full edition is £350 + VAT (2000 prices). But material and prices are changing fast. The British Library publications include several National Curriculum topics such as The Making of the UK, and Medieval Realms, which are excellent for 11–12-year-olds. These will, doubtless, be augmented regularly. AVP is the most common software for schools and has material about the two World Wars and the twentieth century in general. Microsoft Encarta 2000 has a National Curriculum guide and also GCSE subject matter: www.microsoft.com/uk/encarta

See separate reference on **information and communications technology**.

BECTA website: http://vtc.ngfl.gov.uk/resource/cits/history/cd roms.html (for a very full list of CD-ROMs for history and reviews on them).
Cole, M. (1997) *MHR*, **9**(1), September, 16–18.

concept.   A modern replacement for the older word 'idea'. It refers to a class of objects put into a framework. It is a general notion but is not vague. This is exactly where the scientific concept of evolution fits. Sometimes a combination of concepts form an associated pattern, like liberalism, nationalism and socialism, forming a historical pattern of contrasted political philosophies. Language is fundamental to concept, and most concepts are beyond the understanding of a languageless person, although structuralists would suggest that there is a level of understanding which is not wholly associated with the linguistic and is at a different level of perception. A concept is one of the hallmarks of literacy. Concepts much used in history include cause and effect, similarity and difference, and continuity and change. The most important approach to concepts is to try not to misuse or overuse them. The word concept is one of those popular words like 'perception' and 'fascism', which can be used so much and so inaccurately that they lose their true meaning. Arthur Miller expressed this in his play *The Crucible*, written in 1953:

> The concept of unity, in which positive and negative are attributes of the same force, in which good and evil are relative, ever-changing and always joined to the same phenomenon – such a concept is still reserved to the physical sciences and to the few who have grasped the history of ideas.

conservation.   *See separate entry on* **English Heritage***.*

contemporary history.   This has always been a controversial subject because some historians do not believe history can be contemporary or can belong to one's own time. They fear that the essential perspective and proportion which should properly belong to history will be lost if it is concerned with recent events. Other historians, striving for material that will interest students, believe that contemporary history has more appeal.

The *Modern History Review* is the journal of the Institute of Contemporary History and is published by Philip Allen Publishers Ltd, Market Place, Deddington, Oxford OX5 4SE.

Barraclough, G. (1964) *An Introduction to Contemporary History.* London: Watts.

costume.   One of the mirrors of history. 'The clothes of a certain people, of a certain period, of a certain country reflect the moves and customs of a point of history' (Kybalova). Clothes may be considered from the angles of status, taste, profession and the history and climate of the place from which they come. Of particular interest is the slowness of change in costume until visual communication improved and photography became widespread. For example, the corset and the bloomer were more quickly known than the earlier stomacher. In the ancient world it was often only war that enabled different countries to compare or share styles of costume. Nowadays, costume is often dominated by fashion which 'in its widest sense comprises all outward manifestations of civilised behaviour ... such as moral standards, table manners, car designs as well as styles of dress' (*ibid.*).

Liaising with the person in charge of the drama store means that the history teacher or lecturer has a ready supply of useful garments. The other valuable way of introducing students to costume is to take a party to one of the several museums which display garments. The best is the **Bath Museum of Costume**, but it is not unique. Some museums allow students to dress in reproduction period garments.

Kybalova, L. (1966) *The Pictorial History of Fashion*. Feltham, Middx: Hamlyn.
Laver, J. (1974) *A Concise History of Costume*. London: Thames and Hudson.
Mackrell, A. (1997) *An Illustrated History of Fashion*. London: Costume & Fashion Press.
Yarwood, D. (1967) *Outline of British Costume*. London: Batsford.

countryside.   Part of the natural world and also the expression of human endeavour. These have interacted with each other over many centuries. Oliver Rackham writes:

> Trees are not just things that people plant, like gateposts: a friend of mine has cut a good crop of ash trees which have arisen where his predecessor planted pines. The landscape ranges from the almost artificial, like the middle of a barley field, to the almost wholly natural, like the moors of Caithness ... the world of climate, soil and landforms; the world of plants and animals; the world of archaeology; and the world of historical documents ... woods are at the heart of historical ecology, they are inherently stable and long lasting and have outlived many changes in human affairs ... they contain in themselves evidence of at least a thousand years of care and use.

This quotation is from a classic book which tells the story, in minute detail, of the landscape. It is important because all students, whatever their age and the location, are associated with the land in all its forms. There are those experts who can look at a hedgerow and tell you, from what they see, all the things which have happened in that vicinity. Part of this engrossing story comes from the remains which are in the soil, and, of these, pollen analysis tells us almost everything about the wildwood – the natural vegetation of early prehistory – and about the impact of prehistoric men. To quote Oliver Rackham again:

> The historian has to combine the several types of evidence at his disposal ... unfortunately, many historians confine themselves to the written word ... The draining and farming of the Fens in Roman times ... has left not a single written word and is known only from archaeology.

British Ecological Society, Monks Wood Experimental Station, Abbots Ripton, Huntingdon PE17 2LS.

Commons, Open Spaces and Footpaths Preservation Society, 106 Shaftesbury Avenue, London, WC2H 8JH.

Conservation Trust, National Centre for Environmental Education, George Palmer Site, Northumberland Avenue, Reading, Berks RG2 7PW.

Council for the Protection of Rural England, 25–7 Buckingham Palace Road, London SW1 0PP.

Council for the Protection of Rural Scotland, 1 Thistle Court, Edinburgh EH2 1DC.

Countryside Commission, 1 Cambridge Gate, Regent's Park, London NW1 4JY.

Department of the Environment, 2 Marsham Street, London SW1P 3EB.

Forestry Commission, 231 Costorphine Road, Edinburgh EG1 7AT.

AA Book of the British Countryside (1973). London: Drive Publications Ltd (for the Automobile Association).
Hoskings, W. G. (1954) The Making of the English Landscape. London: Hodder and Stoughton.
Rackham, O. (1990) The History of the Countryside. London: Dent.

county record offices.   These vary in quality, but at their best they provide a rich source of archival material which serves as a rich basis for detailed research and a useful resource for document reproduction. It can be encouraging for a student to be able to read a copy of a document that records an important event. It can bring a whole subject to life, and in order to nurture this interest, many record offices make special provision for groups to investigate particular periods. Most contain town and church archives and are therefore crucial in compiling local histories. All archival material should be kept under controlled conditions with regard to temperature and humidity and it is always preferable for documents to be in the care of the record offices. All offices employ an army of researchers who are usually happy to share their knowledge. Staff at the enquiry desk will know who these specialists are, how they can be contacted and whether they have published any material that may be useful to students.

Emmison, F. G. (1966) Archives and Local History. London: Methuen.
Morton, A. and Donaldson, G. (1900) British and National Archives and the Local History. London: Historical Association.

curriculum.   A specified course of study. In the case of history this has to be seen in relation to other subjects in the overcrowded **National Curriculum**. History in the curriculum, as with any other subject, is about balance, proportion and workload. Balance in this context means that there must be an intellectually acceptable disposition between essential categories in the timetable. The categories, or forms of knowledge, are mathematics, physical science, human science, history, philosophy, literature and the fine arts, and religion. Proportion consists of deciding how much teaching time should be allocated to each subject and at what stage. Workload is about ordering students' study commitments so that there is an equal amount of reading or writing, or any other activity, at any stage.

At the time of writing (1999–2000), balance, proportion and workload seem not to be in harmony with each other and this has aroused concern in many quarters. The History Curriculum Association is protesting about the elimination of a proper sense of narrative from history teaching under proposals from the **Qualifications and Curriculum Authority**. This is a cross-curricular organization which replaced the Council of Subject Teaching Associations. The danger is that 'flexibility' is being substituted for a knowledge of landmarks and key people. David Hart, writing in *The Times* (10 August 1999), writes: 'All the kings, queens, heroes, military or otherwise, the majestic march of events, the very stuff and glory of our English history, all of it is to be expunged from our national consciousness.'

Hirst, P. (1974) *Knowledge and the Curriculum*. London: Routledge.

D

Darwin, Charles (1809–82).   Darwin's great work, *On the Origin of Species*, was written in 1859, and put forward the idea of evolution. He argued there had been a natural or a divine explanation for the development of animals, and in the struggle for survival, creatures with advantageous mutations would survive – 'the survival of the fittest', a phrase coined by Herbert Spencer. Darwin held that man had descended from the higher primates and believed that living species were not created individually but had slowly developed over a long period of time – at least five million years. These theories aroused criticism from some Christians and some geneticists, after Mendel had worked on heredity in 1865. Even today, evolution remains a delicate and controversial topic which should always be discussed even-handedly with interpretations being drawn from the students.

The Times (14 August 1999) reported that the Kansas School Board voted to delete evolution from the school curriculum. In another twelve states of the USA, legislation is being passed against the teaching of evolutionary science and, by implication, against a discussion of evolution in any classes.

In 1925 John Scopes was accused of teaching Darwin's theory in a Tennessee school in defiance of state law, and in the following trial the prosecution was led by the former presidential candidate William Jennings Bryan. In the film *Inherit the Wind* Bryan is quoted as saying: 'I am more interested in the Rock of Ages than in the ages of rocks.' Scopes was fined $100 and eventually the verdict was over-turned. The journalist Mencken described Bryan as being transformed into 'A great sacerdotal figure, half man and half archangel – a sort of fundamental pope.' The trial was nicknamed 'The Scope Monkey Trial'.

Social Darwinism interpreted various human social phenomena in the light of evolutionary theory. For example, if the 'fittest' rose to the top, the less successful would cause a degeneration of the species. Social Darwinists conflated social success with reproductive fitness and the conclusions were often misplaced.

> In the past an American's ears were used to keep his spectacles on; with the universal adoption of the contact lens it is probable that evolution may well phase out his ears completely over the next hundred years or so. (Fry, 1992)

Barminster, R. C. (1979) *Social Darwinism*. Philadelphia.
Fry, S. (1992) *Paperweight*. London: Mandarin.
Jones, S. (1999) *Almost Like a Whale*. London: Doubleday (a rewrite of *The Origin of Species*).
Phillips, A. (1999) *Darwin's Worms*. London: Faber.

Dearing Report and Review. Sir Ron (later Lord) Dearing was asked to lead two committees. One was to make the National Curriculum slimmer, more manageable and more easily assessed. The other was to review the nature of qualifications for 16–19-year-olds. Both were accepted and are having powerful results. The Final Report (1994) defined the matter, skills and processes at each Key Stage (*see National Curriculum*).

The review of 16–19 qualifications was published in 1996 and emphasized parity of esteem between academic and vocational education as expressed in the General National Vocational Qualification (GNVQ). The Advanced Subsidiary Level (AS Level) was restructured alongside the introduction of modular courses.

Dearing, R. (1994) *National Curriculum and its Assessment*. London: HMSO.
Dearing, R. (1996) *Review of 16–19 Qualifications* (Final Report). London: SCAA.

debating. Formal discussion with rules of procedure, a given structure and a decisive vote at the end. The proposer of the motion opens the debate and is followed by the principal opposer. The motion being discussed is then 'thrown open' to the assembled people, called the House, named after the House of Commons, from which most of the procedures derive. After the general discussion the summing up begins, starting with the principal opposer, who was the second speaker at the opening. The final speech comes from the proposer of the motion. When this has finished the chairman calls for a vote which is either indicated by a show of hands or else the members file out through two exits and are counted as they do so. The person in the chair is important because the speakers must be summoned in order. They must not speak for too long, and the whole occasion must be handled impartially. In a school or college a debate is a constructive way of introducing a controversial topic because it makes it possible to obtain a balanced view. It also demands that the main participants prepare their speeches, is a convenient way of marshalling complicated or sensitive arguments, offers practice in learning to speak in front of each other and helps students acquire the necessary patience to listen to opposing views. All these acquirable skills are intrinsic to the art of debating.

A famous debate took place in the Oxford Union on 9 February 1933 on the motion: 'This House will in no circumstances fight for its King and Country.' The motion was drafted by the Librarian D. M. Graham and was passed by 275 votes to 153.

Dillon, J. T. (1994) *Using Discussion in Classrooms.* Buckingham: Open University Press.

differentiation. The matching of learning activities to the varying abilities of pupils in a teaching situation. It can be approached in a variety of ways through the use of different teaching strategies, through placing pupils in appropriate groups in the classroom and through using appropriate resources. It is not the same thing as mixed-ability teaching, which seeks to provide for all children at the same time, even if they have a wide range of ability. The differentiation approach tries to group students who have different needs within the same class.

documents. These record information. Any information is precious to the historian (*see archives*; *county record offices*). In his introduction to the Open University course, Conflict and Stability in the Development of Modern Europe 1789–1970, Arthur Marwick suggests a four-fold 'onslaught'. First, there should be a clear and specific identification of the document. Next, the document should be set in its historical context, including the question of its origins, with comment on specific points in the text. Finally, consideration should be given to any consequences arising from its employment. Harriet Jones, in an article in the *Modern History Review* (March 1994), writes that 'traditional textbooks are comfortable, like booking a guided tour through the subject. When looking at primary sources, however, that prop is taken away.' It is often a release to take that prop away, and the use of archives should be a part of the training of every student of whatever age.

See separate entry on **county record offices**.

See separate entry on **Schools Council History Project 13–16**.

Fox, J. (1992) 'Sources: documents'. *MHR*, **4**(1), September.
Jones, H. (1994) 'Sources: interpreting document'. *MHR*, **5**(4), April.
Both **English Heritage** and the **Historical Association** issue a range of documents which are relevant and helpful.

drama. As a part of the curriculum in primary and secondary schools, drama is well established, but there are particular reasons why some find that it has an important place in teaching history. It can 'open doors' of imagination, identification and interest which, for children, are sometimes hard to tap. It can be a genuinely cross-curricular activity and enables students and teachers to collaborate with the widest range of other departments. It is strongly contrasted with many other teaching approaches in history and thus provides variety, emphasis and fun. Much has been written about the value of drama in teaching history.

Paul Goalen and Lesley Hendy (1994) wrote:

> This paper seeks to define the context of providing drama strategies in the teaching of history ... to promote discussion and to clarify ideas and points of view, whilst also enabling teachers to lead children towards a position where they can take on the role of an historian as a commentator on and critic of evidence and interpretations.

H. Caldwell Cook, writing in *The Play Way: An Essay in Educational Method*, in 1917, commented that 'The most well-ordered classes are those in which a body of boy officials has control.' Though old, this book contains many good ideas which ought to be considered afresh.

Fines, J. and Verrier, R. (1974) *The Drama of History*. London: New Univer Education.

Fleming, K. (1992) 'A land fit for heroes: recreating the past through drama'. *TH*, **68**, July.

Goalen, P. and Hendy, L. (1999) 'History through drama'. *Curriculum Journal*, **15**(3), Winter.

Hill, E. B. (1994) 'Project replay: a project designed to show the use of drama in teaching history'. *TH*, **76**, June.

Somers, J. (1991) 'Time capsule: a fusion of drama and history'. *TH*, **64**, July.

Wilson, V. and Woodhouse, J. (1990) *History through Drama*. London: HA.

E

---

emblems. One of the signposts of history. Emblems are pictorial reminders; like the salamander which symbolized François Premier or the skull as the symbol of mortality (*memento mori*) – or the worm of corruption. The eyes and ears on the gowns of Elizabeth I were the emblems of spies. All of these are of great interest and can add colour and meaning to a history topic. They are also aids to the memory; sometimes a student will attach to an emblem a list of valuable associations.

Ashrea, E. M. (1970) *English Emblem Books 1665* (facsimile). Menston: Scholar.
Bath, M. (1993) *Speaking Pictures: English Emblem Books*. London: Longman.

empathy. The power of projecting one's own personality into the object of contemplation. It is part of the affective domain of knowledge. Vivian Little, in an article 'What is historical imagination', in *Teaching History* (June 1983), goes further: 'To say that the historian has perceived, reconstructed, supposed and written with imagination involves saying he has done so with feeling. Excellent history is a masterpiece of art, it is the creative imagination. Let me think of myself, of the thinking being. The idea becomes dim, whatever it be – so dim that I know not what it is; but the feeling is deep and steady, and this I call I-identifying the percipient and the perceived' (*Notebooks*, 1801). Yet the idea of approaching history empathetically has declined in favour over the last fifteen years or so and has always had mixed support. Ann Low-Beer, in an article in *Teaching History* (April 1989), wrote that 'it had to do with feelings, specifically feeling into the spirit, or in an historical context, outlook or millieu of a past historical period'. However, in the same article she quotes an alternative view from Professor Bernard Crick, in his life of George Orwell: 'None of us can enter into another person's mind; to believe so is fiction. We can only know actual persons by observing their behaviour in a variety of different situations and through different perspectives.'

'I feel a feeling which I feel you all feel' (from a sermon by George Ridding, 1885, quoted in G. W. E. Russell, 1898, ch. 29).

Ashy, R. and Lee, P. (1987) 'Children's concepts of empathy and understanding in history', in C. Portal (ed.) *The History Curriculum for Teachers*. London: Falmer.

Fairclough, J. and Redsell, P. (1985) *Living History: Reconstructing the Past with Children*. Colchester: Vineyard.

Lomas, T. (1993) *Teaching and Assessing Historical Understanding*. HA Teaching of History Series, **63**.

Low-Beer, A. (1989) *Empathy and History*. TH, **55**, April, 8–12.

May, T. and Williams, S. (1987) 'Empathy: A case of apathy'. TH, **49**, October, 11–16.

Russell, G. W. E. (1898) *Collections and Recollections*.

Southern Regional Examinations Board (1986) Working Party Report. Southampton: SREB.

Warnock, M. (1976) *Imagination*. London: Faber.

English Heritage.   *See heritage.*

Enlightenment.   This movement pervaded intellectual life in Europe in the eighteenth century. It was founded on the supremacy of reason, religious toleration, scientific advance and literary realism. It was led by men like Goethe and Schiller in Germany (*Aufklarung*); the philosophers and encyclopaedists Diderot, Voltaire, Montesquieu and Rousseau in France; John Locke, Thomas Paine, Isaac Newton in England; and Adam Smith and David Hume in Scotland. Politically, it influenced the growth of revolutionary ideas in France, and it is claimed that the Romantic movement, with its more individual attitudes, was a reaction against the scientific intellectualism represented by the Enlightenment.

Enlightenment thinking may be appreciated after the textual analysis of a suitable passage, for example, the following passage by John Locke (1632–1704), taken from *An Essay Concerning Human Understanding* (1690, book 4, ch. 19, s. 4), repays careful study:

> Reason is natural revelation, whereby the eternal Father of light, and fountain of all knowledge communications to mankind that portion of truth which he has laid within the reach of their natural faculties.

See separate entries on Isaac **Newton** *and Adam* **Smith**.

Erasmus Desiderius (1466–1536).   A major figure in Renaissance humanism and a critic of the Church, Luther and much of the lifestyle of the time. He wanted a peaceful, rational reform of the Church, which would include a reduction of the power of the clergy, but he did not favour the sharp religious conflicts which accompanied many of the controversies of his time. He published several books. *Adages*, published in 1500, was the first printed best-seller and consisted of a collection of proverbs which he started to collect during his visit to Oxford in 1499. *In Praise of Folly*, written in 1511, was a satire on monasticism and the Church, and dedicated to Thomas More. Erasmus lived in Cambridge between 1505 and 1514, and soon after arriving there he published his edition of the Greek text of the New Testament with his own translation in Latin in 1516. His works were placed on the Index of the Council of Trent 1545–63.

Erasmus had an influence in England which arose from his regular visits to London, Oxford and Cambridge. For scholars, clerics and politicians it was like having a regular messenger from the European Renaissance, and while the English did not always agree with him they were at least informed and aware of what was going on on the mainland. His views were independent; he was listened to by all and was one of the main voices of the Renaissance.

Bainton, R. H. (1970) *Erasmus of Christendom*. London: Collins.

evidence.   That which provides proof. In this book there are entries on **archives** and **county records offices**, but evidence involves a wider range of artefacts than could be contained in a record office. Old tools, vehicles, road and building excavations, cemeteries, church memorials, military uniforms and memorabilia, old pens and pencils, costumes and clothes are just some of the items which not only evoke the past but also are intrinsic to the study of it. Such sources become evidence when they are used in an investigation.

One approach to the study of evidence is to approach it like a detective. In David Sylvester's design for the School Council 13–16 History Project he gives every child an artificially created wallet, apparently found in a road accident. The wallet contains a range of information about the person who has been in the accident. The students' task is to find out as much about the person as possible from the wallet. In this way students begin to understand what evidence is and how to use it.

See separate entry on **Schools Council History Project**.

examination approaches.   These can significantly increase the marks which can be obtained in an exam. Although some may decry classes set aside for examination preparation, it is essential to help a student make the most of any talent he or she possesses. This usually involves well-known classroom drills being transferred to the exam room. Time-honoured instructions like to 'read, mark and inwardly digest' remain important. Another rule is to allow time to read the questions carefully before writing an answer. A less popular, but useful, tip is to make a list of proper names and check their correct spellings just before the examination. Last-minute revision should include rehearsing several routines, such as the basic structure of an essay (opening; developed middle section; and conclusion, which ties up any 'loose ends' but does not introduce new material), of document interpretation (read the document; try to understand the main thrust of the passage; and only then start to write an answer) and an accurate recall of phrases and passages learnt by heart during the earlier stages of the course.

Revising facts at the very last moment is inevitable, but it can lead to a lop-sided approach to answering a question. There is a serious risk of jumbling up the facts or losing a sense of balance and structure. One alternative, which sometimes helps to calm the candidate's nerves, is for the teacher or lecturer to make a survey of work which has been undertaken either over the term or over the last few lessons. This helps the student to realize a sense of balance in the course.

Some teachers laugh at mnemonics, or jingles, and some worry because they cannot remember them anyway. Nevertheless, they can be very helpful, and some of us who learned simple rules in arithmetic still rehearse them in approaching sums. It is usually best if students make up their own mnemonics, even if this is meaningless to anyone else.

Once in the examination there are four golden rules: read the paper, read the question, read the answer, read the question again.

expeditions.   Although expeditions are intrinsic to the teaching of history, it is possible to have too many. If they are not used with discretion, the freshness which comes from studying history outside the school or college building will be lost: 'If all the year were playing holidays/To sport would be as tedious as work' (Henry IV, Pt 1, Sc. 2).

The following points should be observed when conducting an expedition:

1. Students should be checked on and off the vehicle.
2. The leader should have a list of the addresses and telephone numbers of everybody in the party, and a note of any special medical requirements.
3. Take travel sickness pills, first-aid kit and water, and allow for lavatory stops en route.
4. Use outside guides wherever possible to allow the students a break from your own voice.
5. Insist the bus arrives on time to avoid any delays in setting off on the trip.
6. Have an itinerary prepared and try to keep to it.

F

family history. The inescapable part of our lives. We all have parents and grandparents, but family history is more than that and, for some, has almost a religious significance. The lives of our own forbears are of great interest, and family history is a time-honoured way of introducing students of all ages to history on a broader canvas. The interest may begin with an investigation of the way grandma lived, but it can sometimes lead to a much wider study of the subject. Family history can therefore be a 'springboard'; and a way of building up experiences of different social and ethnic groups, whilst also being an absorbing subject in its own right.

The work done in historical demography, especially by the Cambridge Group for the History of Population and Social Structure, is of particular note. The work of this group has involved investigations into social structure and the household; the position of the family as an economic and social unit, especially during the Industrial Revolution; and the position of women in society. The aggregation by the group of census returns and parish returns for the whole country has revealed facts about the population in more reliable and comprehensive terms than was previously known.

Cambridge Group for the History of Population and Social Structure, Trumpington Street, Cambridge. Tel: 01223 333181; fax: 01223 333183.

Family Records Centre, 1 Myddleton Street, London EC1R 1VW.

Federation of Family History Societies, The Benson Room, Birmingham and Midland Institute, Margaret Street, Birmingham. Tel: 07041 492032; e-mail: Admin@FFHS.org.uk

Office for National Statistics (formerly Population and Surveys), 1 Drummond Gate, London SW1V 2QQ. Tel: 0207 533 5702; fax: 0207 533 5719.

fascism

Davidoff, L., Doolittle, M., Fink, J. and Holden, K. (1999) *The Family Story*. London: Longman.

fascism.   A difficult concept to explain at any stage, but especially for those hearing it for the first time. A student looks in the dictionary and reads that it is a 'bundle of rods': What has that to do with Mussolini? The dictionary is describing the fasces, or the rods, bound with thongs, which were the sign of authority within and outside Rome. This Roman word 'fasces' was first used by the Fascio di Combattimento in 1919, but it was Mussolini who made Italy the first fascist country and who shaped fascism into a political force. Hitler made comparable changes in Germany. In Italy, as in Germany, the head of the government had total authority over the whole state. He held, as it were, the symbolic 'bundle of rods'. Similar fascist governments to those in Italy and Germany developed in the 1930s in Spain (Falange), Portugal, Austria, Romania (Iron Guard), Croatia (Cagoulards), Hungary (Arrow Cross), France (Croix de Feu), South America and Britain (British Union of Fascists). In all these countries the appeal lay in the order and discipline which the fascist groups represented. Soon, however, they became more military in character and democratic institutions were replaced by a single leader. They thus became totalitarian and were only defeated by military means in World War Two. Although past and present forms of fascism vary, depending in which country they flourish, they are nevertheless all comparable. One of their main characteristics is the lack of intellectual substance to their ideas. They were anti-communist, anti-liberal, paramilitary and often anti-Semitic. They were usually the product of crisis, as in Germany after the Treaty of Versailles, in 1919, and sought to appeal to all classes, which is different, clearly, from communism which is, essentially, a working-class philosophy. 'Fascism is a double-headed monster: a peculiar combination that is radical in form, but reactionary in substance' (Gordon, 1998).

Students are usually fascinated by fascism because of its clear sense of purpose. It is therefore easy to understand, even if one does not agree with its ideas. It is also often flamboyant in style.

Carsten, F. L. (1980) *The Rise of Fascism*. London: Methuen.
Eatwell, R. (1996) *Fascism*. London: Random House.
Gordon, R. (1998) *The Nature of Fascism*. MHR, **9**, March.

federal.   In federal government, power is dispersed between one central and several regional legislatures. Each level of government in a federal system maintains its own institutions, imposes its own laws and taxes and acts directly on the population. It is a difficult political structure to understand and assess. Even the existing examples, though interesting in themselves, are strikingly different from each other yet are still federal. Switzerland is composed of 23 cantons and, of those, three are sub-divided, making a total of 26 administrative units. They have decided, by referendum, to remain neutral and not to join the European Community. These two decisions alone make them distinctive. The United States of America, by contrast, contains 50 states, in a federation devised in 1787. This became the model for Canada, Australia, the Federal Republic of Germany and Yugoslavia, and in all of these there are wide and deep differences.

A profitable way for students to understand federal systems is to use role-play by representing different states in a simulated federal assembly. It matters little what issues are discussed because it is the machinery that should be understood, and so a simulation of the European Community as it might exist if it were to be integrated further would be a suitable model. In such a simulation a group of students representing different European countries could discuss, for example, the Common Agricultural Policy. In this example, the respective national embassies will undoubtedly be very helpful in sending information about their countries and explaining their particular attitudes to the agricultural question. But whatever the topic, the method of simulating the integration of states is a method which helps to enable students to understand the way in which the federal system can work.

Livington, W. S. (1956) *Federalism and Constitutional Changes*. Oxford: Clarendon.

feudal.   The word comes from the Latin noun 'feudum', or 'feodum', which means belonging to the lord. The word 'feudal' became common in Norman England, although a comparable form of feudalism had existed beforehand, and both forms are associated with property held by a landlord in return for rent or service. Feudalism is an abstract term used in the nineteenth century and devised by Sir Thomas Craig and Sir Henry Spelman as a useful but over-simplified way of describing a complicated political and economic system. It has two distinct elements: the weakness of central government and the performance of service in return for land grants (fiefs). The system was operated by the nobility, who held lands from the Crown and, in return, provided troops for the king in times of war. The knight was the tenant of the noble, and villeins lived under his rule. The Church was part of this manorial system and the clergy at all levels were granted their livings from the secular lords and received produce and labour from the peasantry. Eventually the system began to creak when some of the lords built up armies that could rival the king's in their strength and power, and when some of the towns became prosperous enough to seek independence from the tight manorial system controlled by the lord outside their jurisdiction.

Understanding the feudal system is intrinsic to an understanding of the medieval period. Students need to grasp the nature of feudal service, land-holding and serfdom, and then to see all these elements in the context of the times. Egalitarian zeal in attacking slavery will mean that the purpose of the whole structure of feudalism might be obscured. The priorities in medieval society were dictated by the need for stability, food and employment for the price of tribute and subservience. It is worth arguing that this was a fair price to pay. The only way to appreciate the nature of feudalism is to study it and then discuss it; it is an ideal subject for a structured student seminar which should be set in the context of the medieval period in Europe. Feudalism probably originated in the Frankish kingdom during the eighth century and spread into northern Italy, Spain and Germany. The Normans introduced it into England, Ireland, Scotland, southern Italy and Sicily.

Critchley, J. S. (1978) *Feudalism*. London: Allen and Unwin.

films.   These not only give a physical record of a story or an event; they also are important in themselves. For example, Westerns tell the story of the prairie schooners crossing the plains, or the early days of the Gold Rush. The film itself, then, becomes a piece of history, because having been made at a particular time, it tells the story in a manner true to its own period. That is why the early Westerns play so vital a part in telling the history of America; because they tell the story of the early days of cinema as well as portraying their nation's history.

Films create a sense of realism. This is especially true if they contain footage from old newsreels. They also are able to put faces to names, e.g. Peter O'Toole's portrayal of Henry II in *The Lion in Winter* and Queen Victoria as played by Judi Dench in *Mrs Brown*. But it is often items such as costumes and buildings that give a sense of realism, especially if used in brief passages rather than pervading an entire film.

Films act as a bridge between the commercial world and the educational, uncommercial world. Although there are major differences between these two worlds (perhaps because the former has much more money at its disposal) the medium of film can often bring the two together.

For the teacher, films have the distinct advantage of flexibility; it is possible to buy loops of useful shots, or to stop a film and discuss a particular aspect, or to repeat a section if it has particular relevance to a class or a seminar. All of these methods are assets to teaching.

Film Education is a government-sponsored body. Its aims are to promote the use of film in the school curriculum and to further the use of cinemas by schools. It publishes a variety of free teaching materials and organizes visits, lectures and seminars. The organiza-

Freemasonry

tion's address is: Film Education, 41–2 Berners Street, London W1P 3AA.

The British Film Institute is a national agency which has the responsibility for preserving the art of film and television. Its library and information service contains the world's largest collection of published and unpublished material relating to film and TV. It also publishes a useful catalogue. Its address is: 21 Stephen Street, London W1P 2LN. Tel: 0207 255 1444; fax: 0207 436 7950.

Museum of the Moving Image, London SE1 8X7. Tel: 0207 928 3535; fax: 0207 815 1419.

Carnes, M. C. (ed.) (1996) *History According to the Movies*. London: Cassell.
Guy, S. (1994) 'Feature films', *MHR*, **6**(1), September, 16–17.
Law, J. (1998) *Cassell Companion to Cinema*. London: Cassell.
Morris, C. J. (1990) 'Sources: film', *MHR*, **1**(4), April, 11–12.
Walker, J. (ed.) (1999) *Halliwell's Film Guide 2000*. London: HarperCollins.

film strips. These are now out of date and have been superseded by a rich battery of sophisticated electronic aids. Nevertheless, they can be used with effect and need not be rejected totally by the history teacher. They can be used to provide a planned series of pictures on the same subject; for example the Industrial Revolution. The teacher has control over the speed at which slides are shown and can therefore use them to shape the lesson. It would be helpful to have a series of maps when explaining the Peninsular War. Similarly, it is also possible to construct a film strip to suit the particular needs of, say, a local history lesson. Film strips also provide instant contrast should this be required (e.g. to regain students' interests when their concentration has lapsed). A film strip is useful in retracing old ground and this can be helpful in driving a point home. In the world of yesteryear, maximum effect was obtained by using two projectors alternately so that a close-up could accompany the screening of a larger picture. For example, one could look at the tactics of a battle on one screen, and the strategy on another. Although film strips used to be helpful, it is still worth resurrecting them on occasion. Even if the machine itself is not used, the accompanying handbook, which explains the slides, can make interesting reading.

Freemasonry. A society of friends with secrets rather than a secret society. It has an interesting history, although some of the claims about its history would be hard to substantiate. Much has been written about freemasonry, and the subject is included in this book because it is a well-researched example of the medieval and early modern craft guilds. Joint work by G. P. Jones, who was not a freemason, and D. Knoop, who was, makes it clear that there was a strong association between stonemasons, who were building some of the manor houses, cathedrals and castles in the land. It was custom-ary for masons to live together in a hostel, and this would be the first building to be built because of their need of somewhere to sleep and eat. Next they would build the great house or church. Such a community needed social guidelines, a community structure and a set of rules by which to live. Sometimes they made rules that would apply only to themselves because they were protecting their jobs and their future, and so developed a kind of industrial confidentiality. The degree of organization found in stonemasonry can also be found in other craft guilds, though, generally, they were not quite so tightly organized because the members were not living away from home as the stonemasons were.

Students usually find freemasonry interesting because it partly explains one of the 'closed books' of modern society.

Knoop, D. and Jones, G. P. (1933) *The Medieval Mason*. Manchester: Manchester University Press.
Leadbeater, C. W. (1998) *Freemasonry*. London: Grammercy.

free trade.   The free exchange of goods between countries, involv-ing a body of doctrine, principles and instructions. The aim is to encourage growth in the economies of the participating members and it is believed that harmony and a healthy interdependence between those countries will result. The principal exponent of the theory was Adam **Smith** and the group that advocated it was known as the Manchester School. This became increasingly popular by the middle of the nineteenth century and legislation like the Repeal of the Corn Laws in 1846 was enacted. The School was the lynch-pin of much overseas trade and helped England take the lead in industrial innovation, causing it to be nicknamed 'the workshop of the world'. Other countries were challenged by this economic expansion and adopted policies of protectionism, imposing tariffs to protect their industries. The USA, Germany and Australia were prominent in this regard and Britain soon adopted the same policy under Joseph Chamberlain. It became a major factor in British politics when the Ottawa Conference, in 1932, created a limited range of tariffs between Britain and the Dominions. This strengthened the power of the British Empire and the Commonwealth and was opposed by the United States after the Second World War. The USA called a conference in Geneva, in 1947, and the participants agreed to sign a General Agreement on Tariffs and Trade (GATT), which sought to restore a more liberal order. The reductions over the next 30 years helped many economies to grow and encouraged a post-war boom. Britain joined the European Free Trade Association (EFTA) and then the European Economic Community (EEC), and at the same time COMECON was created in Eastern Europe in 1949. World economic diversity in the 1990s led to the creation of the World Trade Organization (WTO) which was meant to enforce GATT rules. What has happened is that other barriers have been erected, such as environmental issues or increased bureaucracy.

Understanding of Britain's place in the trading markets of Europe and the world is inescapable and students need to understand the historical background to trading arrangements.

French Revolution.   This overthrew the Bourbon dynasty, and the *ancien régime* was abolished in 1789. Within three years the monarchy was abolished, the King executed, the republic established and the Reign of Terror had begun. Within ten years Napoleon was emperor, and by 1815 the monarchy, in modified form, was re-established. The first three sentences of this entry focus on the essence of the Revolution, but it explains little about its motives, its permanent effects on France and its massive impact on the world at large. In teaching, it is essential to establish the main features of what happened in France. So often the precise details of the Revolution are explained so ponderously in print, or verbally, that the breathless momentum of what happened is lost in a mass of detail. Therefore, it is vital to give a summary initially, of the main stages of the upheaval. Thereafter students should be encouraged to follow the revolutionary momentum. The Revolution is one of history's greatest stories, and to convey the emotion of the event as well as to impart factual information is the challenge to the teacher.

As with many other historical events there are few better introductions than to visit Paris. Although the demolition of the Bastille occurred on 14 July 1789, as soon as the mob had murdered the governor, the ground plan of the prison is still to be seen, marked by a line of paving-stones, and some of the cellars have survived. The city is full of evocative reminders of the tumult, the régime it replaced, and those which followed.

Bearman, G. (1977) *The French Revolution*. London: Heinemann Educational.
Rosenthal, M. (1965) *The French Revolution*. Harlow: Longman.
Sydenham, M. J. (1969) *The French Revolution*. London: Methuen.

furniture.   The movable contents of a building or room. It is highly individual. Furniture is often ignored by teachers and, consequently, by many students. This is a pity. Some excellent collections exist in museums, like those in the Castle Museum in York, where rooms are set out in authentic period style. Another comparable museum is the Geffrye Museum, situated in Kingsland Road, London E2, which houses permanent displays of fully furnished rooms from Elizabethan times to the 1930s. In both of these museums, as in many others nowadays, children are welcome. In the museums themselves or sometimes in stately homes, which offer the same period flavour, worksheets are very appropriate because they ensure that attention is directed towards those particular artefacts that will dovetail with the school lessons:

> To unite elegance and utility, and blend the useful with the agreeable, has ever been considered a difficult, but an honourable task. There may not be much elegance in the classroom but there can be much harmonious utility; it would also be a desirable aspiration to 'blend the useful with the agreeable'. (Hepplewhite, in his preface to *The Cabinet-Maker and Upholsterers Guide*)

Students should be encouraged to look critically at the furniture which is all around them and perhaps start a notebook listing what they have seen. It is also helpful to compile a scrapbook of cuttings and photographs which might be the first step to recognizing the different historical periods and might also engender a life-long interest in the subject.

Beard, G. (1985) *English Furniture*. London: Viking.
Edwards, R. and Ramsey, L. G. G. (1961) *The Connoisseur Period Guides*. London: .
Fastnedge, R. (1955) *English Furniture Styles 1500–1830*. London: Penguin.

G

Gandhi. Mohandas Karamchand Gandhi (1869–1948) was a great Indian political leader who became the architect of his country's independence and a prophet of non-violence throughout the world. He claimed that he had 'nothing new to teach the world. Truth and non-violence are as old as the hills.' In a world where pacifism and nuclear disarmament are ever more prevalent forces in society, there is continuing support for Gandhi's ideals. He ate sparingly, wore home-spun clothes and walked whenever he could. He was environmentally-friendly, humble, effective politically and is still an icon over 50 years after his death.

Gandhi was imprisoned in the Aga Khan Palace in Poona, and there is a memorial there which includes the following quotation written and signed by him:

> A born democrat is a born disciplinarian. Democracy comes naturally to him who is habituated normally to yield willing obedience to all laws, human or divine. Let all those who are ambitious to serve democracy qualify themselves by satisfying first this acid test of democracy. Moreover, a democrat must be utterly selfless. He must think and dream not in terms of self or party but only of democracy. Only then does he acquire the right of civil disobedience. I do not believe that a healthy and honest difference of opinion will injure our cause. But opportunism, camouflage or patched up compromises certainly will. If you must dissent you should take care that our opinions voice your innermost convictions and are not intended merely as a convenient party cry.

A synopsis of Gandhi's life is available in extended or potted form in all the standard biographical summaries. His autobiography was first published in 1927 and has been reprinted many times. The *Standard Life*, by Louis Fischer, was first published in 1950. The film *Gandhi* is also readily accessible.

Gandhi, directed by Richard Attenborough, Columbia Pictures, 1982.

gender. Quite different from sex. Gender refers to the social and cultural differences between men and women. The word comes from the Latin *genus*, which means a sort or a kind. Gender has come to mean all the differences between men and women which are not physical; the physical are described as sexual differences. That Queen Elizabeth I was a sovereign queen describes a gender differentiation, but that she was the Virgin Queen describes a sexual characteristic. Some cultural indicators make no gender or sexual distinctions. For example, some of the languages of the North American Indians have two 'genders', animate and inanimate, and take no account of sex.

The history teacher must be sensitive to the aspect of gender. To teach about outstanding women only, for example – Boadicea, Elizabeth I, Elizabeth Fry, Madame Curie – and give the impression that in times past there were the same opportunities for women as there were for men is to distort the truth. To teach only that life was hard for women is to ignore the important role many women played in society. What is required is to explain the unbalanced nature of many societies as dispassionately as possible, and to do it through the eyes of those alive at the time, not through the eyes of modern commentators. For example, some farmers' wives in Dorset, in the nineteenth century, were responsible for running a farmhouse, running two barns, furnished like dormitories, with young men in one and young women in the other, and being in charge of the dairy side of the farm as well. Yet they had no security of tenure and no recourse if their husbands decided to remove them from the homestead. Women had important and responsible managerial roles, but were, at the same time, not secure financially. To represent a balanced view of this situation, the role of the man must also be explained and the nature of his tenure described as well as his managerial position in relation to his staff.

Coward, R. (1999) *Sacred Cows: Is Feminism Relevant to the Next Millennium?* London: Collins.
Gender and Development. Published three times a year by Oxfam, 274 Banbury Road, Oxford OX2 7DZ.
Gender and Society. Official publication of Sociologists for Women in Society.

General Certificate of Education. The GCE (Ordinary Level) was introduced in 1951 to replace the School Certificate and was designed for the top 20–30 per cent of children.

General Certificate of Secondary Education. The GCSE replaced the GCE, as well as the Certificate of Secondary Education (CSE), in 1986 by creating one examination for all 16-year-old pupils, taken after a two-year course of study.

*See separate entry on the **National Curriculum**.*

General National Vocational Qualification. The GNVQ, introduced in 1992 for students who wished to go into employment or to university, has parity with the GCSE and is an examination based on attainment, unlike the NVQ which is based on vocational competences. A new style of unit was introduced in 2000 in all GNVQ subjects at Foundation, Intermediate and Advanced levels. The new units set out the knowledge, understanding and skills required in clear, jargon-free language. At all levels, the qualification consists of a combination of compulsory and optional units. At Foundation and Intermediate levels, three out of six units are compulsory; at Advanced level, from six to eight of the units studied are compulsory, appropriate to the vocational area. At Advanced level, a new six-unit GNVQ has been introduced. Three or four of the units will be compulsory, appropriate to the vocational area. The six-unit GNVQ has been designed to meet progression needs in different vocational areas and offers choice and flexibility to schools and colleges. Evidence from piloting indicates that this qualification adds to the breadth of students' programmes.

At the time of writing, Advanced level, a new, three-unit GNVQ is mooted for September 2000. If introduced it will be available in a very limited range of titles in specific vocational areas where the demand from employers, schools and colleges is clear and where the award represents a coherent qualification.

Assessment. The assessment arrangements for GNVQ are designed to increase rigour and manageability. Normally, one-third of the assessment is external. External assessment may take a number of forms, such as set assignments or tests administered by awarding bodies, depending upon the unit being assessed. The remaining two-thirds of the assessment, that is internal, is moderated by the awarding body. Assessment and grading are based on performance in the unit using assessment criteria based on the unit's requirements. Evidence from the pilot indicates that the new model – streamlined in the light of experience – is considerably more reliable, accurate and manageable.

Grading. Each unit is graded. Unit grades are converted into points, which are aggregated to produce a grade for the whole qualification. At Intermediate and Foundation level, pass, merit and distinction grades are used. At Advanced level, A–E grading is used, in line with the A-Level system. This gives selectors in higher education, and employers, more information and makes it easier for them to compare candidates' performances across different qualifications.

Part One GNVQ. This consists of three compulsory units (at the time of writing) at Intermediate and Foundation levels. It is available nationally in seven areas with new units available from September

2000. It is also available at Post-16 level. For more information, contact the 14–19 Curriculum Section at **Qualifications and Curriculum Authority**.

Key Skills. Key Skills are essential features of government plans for the education and training of 16–19-year-olds. A qualification based on the key skills of communication, application of number and information technology became available in September 2000. Attainment is assessed and recorded separately on a single certificate for students who achieve a level in all three skills. GNVQ qualifications are awarded on the basis of attainment in the vocational units, with attainment in the Key Skills being reported separately and certified as indicated above. Key Skills nevertheless remain an integral part of teaching and learning in all GNVQ programmes. At AS and A Level, where a Key Skill is integral to attainment in the subject, specific assessment requirements are included, and contribute directly to the grades awarded. The Key Skills are signposted clearly in the GNVQ vocational units. A similar approach applies to A Levels. A-Level study encourages students to generate portfolio evidence that can be used in the Key Skills qualification or can contribute to achievement of individual Key Skills units. This approach is designed to encourage all students studying at A Level to exploit opportunities to develop Key Skills in the context of their studies. Where their studies do not generate all the evidence needed for Key Skill certification, evidence from other sources is required. The wider Key Skills of improving own learning and performance, working with others and problem-solving continues to be part of post-16 education and training programmes. GNVQ and A-Level courses provide opportunities for the development of these skills. These opportunities are also signposted in A-Level and GNVQ specifications. The Key Skills Qualification is available nationally, having been implemented phasically from September 1999. It is not compulsory for A/AS Level, nor for those doing GNVQ or Single Award GNVQ. It is compulsory for Modern Apprenticeships and National Traineeships. All A/AS-Level specifications include some information about the opportunities for the development of Key Skills. At the time of writing, the final assessment model is not yet decided, but there should be no conflict with the courses of study followed by A-Level candidates. Key Skills can be covered by following a General Studies A-Level course, because of the cross-curricular nature of both.

Quicke, J. (1999) 'Key Skills and the "Learning Curriculum"'. *Forum*, **41**(1), 35.

glasnost and perestroika.   Two words associated with the thawing of relations between east and west. Glasnost means openness, loosening up and acting publicly in everything. Perestroika means restructuring or rebuilding and was an internal social and economic process. The great apostle in the USSR was Mikhail Gorbachev, who became President of the USSR in March 1985, having been previously General Secretary of the Communist Party. He had shown little indication that he was to become such an enlightened international statesman in the early stages of his career and had supported Brezhnev when he had crushed the Czech rising, and also Andropov when he did the same in Hungary. When he became Head of State, however, he withdrew Soviet troops from Afghanistan, scaled down the war in Central America and endorsed peace moves in Southern Africa and South-East Asia. He permitted Eastern Europe's liberation, ended the Communist Party's monopoly of power in Russia and appeared ready and willing to end the Cold War. He agreed to the demolition of the Berlin Wall and also the reunification of Germany. However, he did not concede to the aspirations of the Baltic republics of Latvia and Lithuania, nor to other attempts at breaking away from centralized control in other parts of the USSR. In all these different areas he made the world appear more peaceful, and sought to increase harmony between nations.

Students find it hard to think of the Cold War, the Iron Curtain and the implacable ideological divisions which existed before Gorbachev came to power, because outside the old USSR these are largely alien concepts. One approach is to make a biographical contrast between Gorbachev and Kruschev and to reduce the monolithic politics of the central European past to the personal traits of the leaders. Another, easier approach is to show video tapes of military actions of the Russian forces and use them as the starting point for a general discussion. During the period of glasnost and perestroika there were large numbers of cartoons produced which are revealing as well as humorous, and they provide an interesting collection of documents for analysis.

It is necessary to mention that support inside and outside the Soviet Union was by no means universal. Many Russians were suspicious of glasnost and of Gorbachev; Sovietskaya Kutura commented: 'Support for Gorbachev is by no means general or unanimous or always sincere.'

gramophone records. Now of minor importance compared to tapes and **compact discs**, but they have some value. One should ensure that the player is in good working order. It is an even richer experience if the record is played in tandem with an old silent movie on a portable gramophone. There is something fascinating about the feel of old records; they contrast sharply with modern equivalents. Such items engender a strong sense of history.

Selecting and storing old records is not always possible for a school or college. The British Library, in Euston Road, has a permanent facility for listening to 78 rpm records.

Martland, P. (1995) 'Sources: gramophone records'. *MHR*, **7**(2), November, 23–5.

group work.   Intrinsic to all history teaching. It tries to suggest ways of teaching groups of four to six, where several such groups make up the class. In some mixed-ability teaching, groups of approximately five students are commonplace and usually comprise children of roughly equal ability.

Splitting into small groups can promote genuine participation and sharing. A class of 13-year-olds, working on the life and career of Napoleon, could profitably split up into groups and each attempt to explore one aspect. When this analysis is completed, a subsequent plenary session may enable each group to report its findings. Alternatively, written reports of each group's work could be displayed in a classroom exhibition. Following either of these approaches, the class could write a general view of the life of Napoleon, and there will have been considerable opportunity to work together in the process.

In such a fragmented setting, discipline can only be maintained if the students are enjoying the subject. Work must be marked meticulously. The marking and discussion of work is often the only personal contact the student will have with the teacher, and the student will usually respond positively if marked work is returned promptly.

'The children were participating in an altogether freer situation than occurs in a formal class lesson' (Kaye and Rogers, 1994). 'We writers all act and react on one another; and when I see a good thing in another man's book I react on it at once' (Leacock, 1922).

*See separate entries on **differentiation** and **mixed-ability teaching**.*

Kaye, B. and Rogers, I. (1994) *Group Work in Secondary Schools.* Oxford: OUP.
Kutnich, P. and Rogers, C. (1994) *Groups in Schools.* London: Cassell.
Leacock, S. (1922) *My Discovery of England.* London.

guerrilla.   The Spanish word for a little war. It means an irregular war carried out by small groups of people acting independently. The word was first used during the Peninsular War (1807–14) and is described by Richard Ford (1796–1858), who spent years making riding tours of Spain and who published a *Handbook for Travellers in Spain* in 1845, which colourfully describes the way the fighters worked. Another example is the Resistance fighters during the Second World War.

The IRA are also guerrilla fighters and carry out irregular warlike missions both in Ireland and on the English mainland. They are an army, but one which avoids full-scale confrontation, while keeping the English enemy under pressure.

History is full of examples of guerrilla war. A good example is Lawrence of Arabia who fought in the Middle East between 1916 and 1918. Perhaps the most sustained and effective example comes from the guerrilla activities of Mao Tse Tung, who fought against the Kuomintang and the Japanese, an activity which played an important part in the unification of communist China. In this example, guerrilla warfare became the instrument of ideological and national cohesion. Che Guevara (1928–67), however, must remain the great strategist of guerrilla war and the icon for so many revolutionary movements in South America.

Such hostilities, sadly, are a recurring feature of the modern world, and are unlikely to disappear, even if more conventional war becomes less frequent. It is therefore helpful to study previous occurrences. Much material is available for this purpose. The Imperial War Museum (*see* **museums (London)**) has, on display and for sale, a range of posters and other material which would enhance any lesson.

H

handbook. The history department handbook should be an honest expression of what the department stands for and the ways in which it is accountable. It is particularly useful for teachers of other subjects who are drafted in to teach classes and it is vital for student teachers working in the department.

The handbook should explain what the department represents and should be the shared written record of thought and discussion by all members of the department, not just the person at the head of it. It should help everybody, inside and outside the department, to know what everybody else is doing and for what they are striving.

The handbook should include the following headings: an introduction; a statement of aims; a statement of the ways the subject is taught (methodologies); policies; schemes of work; and, finally, a catalogue of resources available.

The introduction must say what the handbook is about, give reasons for studying history and explain in general terms the department's approach to the subject. It should outline which subjects and which skills are taught at which stage. Particular attention should be paid to ICT, and teachers should not assume that all children know all there is to know about computers. The aims should address the question of why we teach history. Methodology would occupy the major part of the book; if the department has particular preferences this is where they should be stated. The policy section should contain agreed statements on assessment, classroom management, **differentiation**, equal opportunities, homework, ICT, initial teacher training, INSET, OFSET, marking and visits. Schemes of work outline what the department does; they should include objectives, topics, concepts, activities and assessment.

Hegel. Georg Hegel (1770–1831) lectured on the philosophy of history in the University of Berlin which was, in 1830, the intellectual centre of the German states. He wrote:

> In history, we are concerned with what has been and what is; in philosophy, however, we are concerned not with what belongs exclusively to the past or to the future, but with that which is, both now and eternally – in short, with reason. (*Lectures on the Philosophy of World History*, 1830, trans. H. B. Nisbet, 1975, p. 94)

He believed that history had meaning and a direction we can discern: 'The history of the world is none other than the progress of the consciousness of freedom.' His conception of freedom is central to his thought. Real freedom comes when we can control the forces which have controlled us and starts with the capacity of human beings to reason. Then a community can be founded on a rational basis and our duty and self-interest will coincide. Other approaches to freedom in which the person is left alone, not interfered with and 'Able to choose as I please' (J. S. Mill) are irrational.

Hegel would never have regarded the kind of state set up by Stalin or Hitler as a rational state, with free citizens, because it ignored his concept of spirit or mind (*geist*), which was central to his philosophy. Marx did not accept *geist*, and substituted materialism and class-conscious philosophy. Marx, however, takes much of Hegel's thought and embraces it. For example, the familiar dialectic of thesis, antithesis and synthesis is Hegelian, but was fully incorporated by Marx and became a strategy for changing capitalism. Through this particular thrust of communist theory and practice, Marx believed that society would be changed and thus the interests of the individual and the community would be in complete harmony.

A separate entry on the **philosophy of history** considers several other major philosophers, but Hegel has been highlighted because of his close connection with Marx.

Singer, P. (1983) *Hegel*. Oxford: OUP.

heraldry. Heraldry is the word used to describe a collection of devices, armorial bearings and heraldic symbolism. The word 'herald' is derived from the Anglo-Saxon 'here' (an army) and 'wald' (strength or sway), but it might have come originally from the German word 'Herold'. Only the head of the family bears the ancestral coat of arms. It can indicate part of the history of that family, and in some aristocratic examples, such as the Cecils, the Bowes-Lyons or the Montague-Scotts, it can be revealing. The latter is the family of the Duke of Baccleuch, and the main line has a royal link through the Duke of Monmouth, the illegitimate son of James II, who married into the family. If, through successive generations, members of a family marry persons entitled to bear arms, more complex shields result, incorporating as many as nine, or even more, coats of arms.

Armoury comes within the scope of heraldry and is the science of the rules and laws governing the use, display and meaning of the pictured signs and emblems on a shield, helmet or banner.

> The boast of heraldry, the pomp of pow'r
> And all that beauty, all that wealth e'er gave,
> Awaits alike the inevitable hour:
> The paths of glory lead but to the grave.
> (Thomas Gray (1716–71) 'Elegy written in a Country Churchyard')

The College of Arms (Heralds College), Queen Victoria Street, London EC4. Tel: 0207 248 2762. (The college strictly governs the rules about the composition and the construction of a coat of arms.)

Fox-Davies, A. C. (1956) *A Complete Guide to Heraldry* (6th edn). London: Nelson.
Spurrier, P. (1997) *The Heraldic Art Source Book*. London: Blandford.

heritage.   English Heritage is the major agency for urban and rural regeneration in all regions of England. It is 'a story of managed change; of innovative, conservation-led ... regeneration projects all over the country which are contributing to our urban and rural renaissance' (from *Heritage Dividend*, published by English Heritage, London, 1999).

English Heritage is the Government's statutory adviser on all aspects of the historic environment. It is actively concerned with conservation and works through nine regional centres. English Heritage believes conservation-led change has a vital role to play in the social and economic regeneration of our towns and cities, and the creation of safe, stable and sustainable communities. Students will be able to find a project in their own area.

English Heritage is concerned also with post-war architecture: buildings such as the Chichester Festival Theatre 1960–2, the Snowdon Aviary in London Zoo (1962–5) and the National Recreation Centre at Crystal Palace (1960–4) are considered, alongside planned town centres such as the shopping parades in Lansbury, London E14 (1949–51) and rural housing, e.g. 1–30 Windmill Green, Ditchingham, Norfolk (1947–9). There is also the evaluation, recording and management of twentieth-century military sites such as Dunkeswell Airfield in Devon or the GHQ Reserve in Oxfordshire.

Brochures and illustrative material can be obtained from: English Heritage, 23 Saville Row, London W1X 1AB. Tel: 0207 973 3000; website: http://www.english-heritage.org.uk

East Midlands – 0845 3010 005; Eastern – 0845 3010 006; London – 0845 3010 009; North East – 0845 3010 001; North West – 0845 3010 002; South East – 0845 3010 008; South West – 0845 3010 007; West Midlands – 0845 3010 004; Yorkshire and Humberside – 0845 3010 003.

Historical Association. Founded in 1906, 'to bring together people who share our interest in, and love for the past'. Membership of HA is open to all. It publishes an *Annual Bulletin of Historical Literature*, the quarterly, illustrated, *The Historian, History, Primary History* and *Teaching History*. It runs conferences, seminars, tours, lectures and events around the country, in association with its 69 branches.

The *General History* pamphlets are particularly helpful for teachers and lecturers. The journal *Teaching History* is for teachers of 11–19-year-olds; published quarterly it covers all aspects of history teaching at Key Stage 3, GCSE and Post-16.

The Historical Association, 59a Kennington Park Road, London SE11 4JH. Tel: 0207 735 3901; fax: 0207 582 4989; website: www.history.org.uk; e-mail: enquiry@history.org.uk

historical demography. Demography is the study of population. It involves the study of statistics relating to births, marriages, deaths, disease and any others which illustrate conditions of life in communities of the past. The population census was introduced in 1801 and provided a more reliable basis for recording size and composition of the population. Previously, parish registers were the main recorders of population statistics, and although this evidence was helpful, it was inaccurate. Nevertheless, the collation of parish registers enabled a random sample of population records to be compiled. This was, for all its imperfections, valuable research, notably that carried out by Wrigley, Schofield and Laslett. This work has continued since the 1970s and continues to be centred on the Cambridge Group on the History of Population based in Trumpington Street, Cambridge.

One of the techniques used in population study is aggregative analysis, which is the quantitative measuring of variables. This can be concerned with fertility, mortality, family and size of population. It is also much used by economic historians in the investigation of industrial output and income as an expression of the national economy. There is, therefore, often a significant overlap between the work of the historian and that of the economist. For example, does the output of a factory have any relationship to the size of the workers' families?

Students can gain a great deal from the study of local census returns which are often ignored by local historians and by teachers.

Local population statistics constitute a rich store of historical information which is easy to access and interpret. Less obvious sources of information reside in school records. When these show variations in the number of pupils this is often due to changes in the nature of education or employment in that area. This kind of research is one way in which history can become 'real'.

historiography. The way history is written. Over the centuries there have been many different ways of doing it. For some, like Sima Qian (145–85 BC), who was the 'Father of Chinese History', it consisted of being able to look at imperial history and interpret bronzes. For medieval and Renaissance historians it was being able to emulate the standards and quality of the writings of ancient Romans like Tacitus, Livy and Suetonius. Much medieval writing was done by priests because they were the literate minority. However, by the time of Gibbon, the practices were changing and his approach was more rational and interpretative. Neibuhr (1776–1831), and Ranke (1795–1886) tried to explain how history actually happened. They used primary evidence and began the first serious steps in the critical evaluation of the material. **Marx** wrote with one consistent aim, which was to interpret change through the class struggle. Marc Bloch (1836–1944) widened this by discussing 'total history', which he saw as being an understanding of the way people act.

See separate entry on the **philosophy of history**.

Hitler. Chosen for special mention because his life affords a good, though not unique, chance to study prejudice on the one hand, and a fascinating life on the other. The actions and effects of Hitler are a cocktail of horror, cruelty, power and hyper-efficiency.

Hitler gave Germany back its sense of pride after the crushing terms of the Versailles Treaty. He created full employment, extended the frontiers to include all German-speaking peoples and won the support of leaders outside Germany including the British Prince of Wales, the French leader, Laval and the Norwegian leader, Quisling, who became his puppet during the 1939–45 War. The majority of German people supported Hitler completely.

Hitler offers a good example of the difficulties that can be experienced in trying to be balanced in making assessments. The historian must try to neutralize negativity and prejudice.

Bullock, A. (1990) *A Study in Tyranny*. Harmondsworth: Penguin.

Hitler, A., *Mein Kampf* (ed. and trans. R. Manheim). London: Watts.
Kenshaw, I. (1998) *Hitler.* Harmondsworth: Penguin.

Holocaust. A Greek word meaning, like *shoah*, the Hebrew equivalent, catastrophe. It was an ordeal suffered by the Jews in Nazi Europe between 1933 and 1945. In the first part of this period various anti-Semitic laws were passed by which Jews lost citizenship rights, the right to hold office, practise professions, inter-marry with Germans or avail themselves of public education. Their property was registered and Jews were often attacked violently. Official propaganda encouraged 'true' Germans to hate and fear Jews. Consequently many Jews fled Germany. The second phase involved concentration camps, forced labour and mass exterminations. A master plan was agreed at the Wannsee Conference in January 1942 and administered by Adolf Eichmann (1906–62). As a result of this savage policy the death toll was horrific and over two-and-a-half million Jews died in Poland alone. Hitler believed that the Jews, as well as gypsies and homosexuals, were a threat because they would inter-marry with 'pure-blooded' Germans and they would exploit the economy.

Students need to understand the force and horror of the Jewish plight. Time sometimes obscures the sharp edges of terror, but the Holocaust is one human tragedy which it behoves us to remember in order to avoid the possibility of any such repetition. Andreas Hoffmann, who is a tour guide at Sachsenhausen Concentration Camp, in the town of Oraienburg, was interviewed for *The Times* in October 1999 and said: 'Some people still refuse to believe the holocaust happened. It is very sad ... It was not just used for the killing of Jews but many other groups as well ... It is a lesson in man's inhumanity.' In *The Sunday Times* of 24 October 1999 there was an account of the world's first museum dedicated to the history of the Third Reich at Obersalzberg which was the site of Hitler's Bavarian holiday home. Mr Dahm, a spokesman, said: 'This is the first permanent exhibition in the world which shows the whole face of the Third Reich and not just a sector such as the Resistance or the Holocaust.'

It may be helpful for students to write an account of life in a Jewish ghetto. *The Diary of Ann Frank* helps to explain the trauma of it.

The Holocaust Education Trust produces a holocaust pack designed for the secondary school teacher and includes a video, maps, flash cards, reproduction documents and teaching notes.

38 Great Smith Street, London SW1P 3BU. Tel: 0207 222 6822; fax: 0207 233 0161; website: www.her.org.uk

Adelman, A. and Lapides, R. (1989) *Lodz Ghetto: Inside a Community Under Siege.* London: Viking.
Davies, I. (2000) *Teaching the Holocaust.* London: Cassell.
Gilbert, M. (1999) *Holocaust.* London Holocaust Educational Trust.

housing. It is comparable in importance to **family history** because it is possible to learn from other members of the family what their houses were like, and thus one can get an impression of the social history of an area. Sometimes, in communities where a family has been settled for a long time, the story of the houses in which they lived can become a checklist of major events in national history, and the development of housing estates around any large city is often an indication of important changes in local society. The Local History section of the local library can be a valuable resource.

There is a wealth of historical records available which can prevent the study of housing from becoming merely anecdotal. Many early problems had come from the massive, unplanned housing schemes which exploded in the nineteenth century. These were caused by the expansion of industry and the migration of country people into the towns. Various philanthropists, such as Octavia Hill and George Peabody, sought to improve the slum housing conditions which had developed, and launched various schemes, such as the promotion of 'model dwellings'. At the same time, writers like Dickens were also highlighting the squalor which existed in the cities. Very slowly, housing management principles were emerging and these were refined after the two world wars with the provision of local authority housing and other ways of providing acceptable domestic accommodation for large numbers of people.

humanities. An integrated conglomeration of associated subjects, usually including history. Some people have always believed that the humanities should have a place in the curriculum, and there is much to be said in favour of this. However, considerable pressure has been placed upon available teaching time because of the increased demands of the National Curriculum.

From an intellectual point of view most arts subjects combine easily; in the Peninsular War, for example, the relationship between geography and history is clear, and necessary to an understanding of the battle strategies in the campaign. The plateau is deeply dissected by rivers and therefore presents serious difficulties in the movement of soldiers. Wellington realized this, but Napoleon did not. In this example, as in others, the teacher should attempt to cover the whole story without artificial subject barriers being drawn.

'Animosities are mortal, but the Humanities live for ever' (Christopher North, 1785–1854, in *Blackwood's Magazine*, August 1834: Notes Ambrosiana number 67).

Little, V. and Campbell, J. (eds) (1989) *Humanities in the Primary School*. London: Falmer.

Mial, D. S. (ed.) (1990) *Humanities and the Computer*. Oxford: Clarendon.

Rudduck, J. (1983) *Schools Council Humanities Curriculum Project Revised*. University of East Anglia.

human rights.   On 10 December 1948 the General Assembly of the United Nations adopted and proclaimed the Universal Declaration of Human Rights. It declares that all human beings are born free and equal and are entitled to the rights and freedoms in the Declaration without discrimination on grounds of race, colour, sex, language, politics or religion. The rights enumerated include civil rights like freedom of expression, conscience, movement, peaceful assembly and association, and economic and social rights involving work, an adequate standard of living, education and participation in cultural life.

Council of Europe (1995) *Human Rights*. Strasbourg Council of Europe.
Owen, D. (1978) *Human Rights*. London: Jonathan Cape.
Wadham, J. (1999) *Blackstone's Guide to the Human Rights Act 1998*. London: Blackstone.
  (Includes a copy of the Act.)

I

ideology.   Refers to a political belief system. It was given particular currency by Marx who analysed society through a system of social class. It is now used more narrowly, and usually refers to a normative group of beliefs or ideas held by an individual or a group. This contrasts with an epistemic approach such as that of the Jesuits.

Eagleton, T. (1991) *Ideology.* London: Verso.

imperialism and colonialism.   Imperialism is the system which administers an empire, under which one country is subordinate to another. A staged-format debate gives a chance to consider the pros and cons of colonialism. There are valid arguments on both sides: for example, it would be easy for a communist to defend the extension of Soviet influence in Eastern Europe after the 1939–45 War, because of the economic benefits and the stability, that ensued. Such arguments are also the ones which could be used to justify the British Raj in India.

   The debate would then hinge upon various important distinctions and definitions. Is imperialism the same as colonialism? What is the precise definition of imperialism? Does the definition necessarily imply subjugation and exploitation? A debate on these lines is likely to be stimulating enough to encourage independent reading.

   'If it were necessary to give the briefest possible definitions of imperialism we should have to say that it is the monopoly stage of capitalism' (Lenin, 1915, ch. 7). 'All the same, sir, I would put some of the colonies in your wife's name' (Joseph Hertz, Chief Rabbi to George VI, quoted in Chips Cannon's diary, 3 June 1943).

See separate entry on the **scramble for Africa**.

Hobson, J. A. (1902) *Imperialism.*
Judd, D. (1996) *The British Imperial Experience from 1765 to the Present.* London: Basic Books.
Lenin, V. (1915) *Imperialism as the Highest Stage of Imperialism.*

Lichtheim, G. (1971) *Imperialism*. London: Allen Lane.

indigenous people. These are important in history teaching because they often represent a world that is lost. At best, indigenous peoples can represent a 'world in miniature', at worst only a minor curiosity. The Ainu are the indigenous people on the island of Hokkaido in Japan. They try to represent the true harmony between people and nature and see animals as incarnations of gods. They were, and are, hunter-gatherers but there are now fewer than a hundred pure-blooded Ainu left. In looks, language and traditions they are unlike any other Asian culture. They have their own dance modelled on that of the Japanese crane. Foxes are credited with supernatural powers; eagles are old friends; crows are respected for boldness; swans are believed to be ancestors, and so on.

Nunavut is the newest Canadian territory inhabited by the Inuit. Maoris, who live in New Zealand, now enjoy full political rights after a stormy political disagreement with the British. North American Indians are spread throughout the continent and organized in tribes – Iroquois (north-east), Cherokee (south-east), Comanche (Great Plains), Apache (desert west), Painte (far west), Chinook (Pacific North-west), Nez Perce (Mountain).

Aborigines are the indigenous Australoids. The population was estimated at 500,000 in 1788 but has now dropped to about 50,000. There has been a cultural resurgence since 1948 with consequent demands for social and cultural equality.

Bates, D. (1966) *The Passing of the Aborigines*. London: John Murray.

Industrial Revolution. The nineteenth-century revolution in industry consisted of a major increase in the number of mills, mines, factories and other such workplaces, with a consequent increase in the expansion of the workforce in the towns. Output and productivity increased greatly and were often associated with developments and technologies in water power, steam power and the use of coal. These developments, and others, transformed Glasgow, the North, the Midlands and parts of Wales, especially in the south. Such expansion was the product of market opportunities, political stability and inventiveness. Nevertheless, although Britain pioneered many of these developments, industrial productivity soon became higher in Germany and the USA. The new skills may have changed the face of Britain but they also changed the face of the world, and continue to do so.

The Industrial Revolution is a subject for all ages and all regions. For areas like Lancashire and Yorkshire the effects of the changes are still there to see: the derelict or converted factories, the terraced housing and the impressive corporation buildings. The trams, the smoke and the polluted rivers have disappeared, but there are new symbols to be detected: the modern industrial estates; the clean, spacious and carefully planned housing developments, including blocks of flats; the comprehensive schools; and the vandalism, addiction and social dysfunction within the community. Some argue that the Industrial Revolution has never ended but that it has only changed its form. Consequently, the history of the Revolution remains important.

Arkwright, Boulton, Cort, Crompton, Hargreaves, Kay, Watt and Wedgewood can be enhanced with visits that can help to sustain interest and imagination. One of the best centres is at Ironbridge in Telford which has been restored as a model nineteenth-century town and is partly run by schoolchildren in period costume.

Barton, A. (1983) *Our Industrial Past*. London: Philip for Natural Trust.

information and communication technology. ICT includes word-processing, text-processing, spreadsheets, mapping, modelling (hypothesis formation), databases, desk-top publishing, interactive television, CD-ROMs and the Internet. Systems like Microsoft Access and Database Management Systems (DBMS) are able to analyse, sort and store a vast amount of data. They are also 'relational', which means they define relationships between categories of data which are included in the structure of the database. Peter Denley and Manfred Thaller developed a revolutionary Relationship Database Management System, called Kleio, which is one of the first custom-made pieces of software designed for historians in Britain. Other pioneer work in history is being spearheaded by the **Institute of Historical Research**. Text-processing has seen developments in the adaptation of concordance programmes, the most common being the Oxford Concordance Package (OCP), which test the reliability of documents and can accommodate the source analysis of large volumes of text. All of Gladstone's speeches, for example, can be accessed.

The Internet is a worldwide network of computers all linked together via telephone lines. It is a network that carries data between computers. But it is not just about computers; it is about people talking and sharing information. Many services are available, such as e-mail, joining discussion groups and looking at pages on the World Wide Web. British government ministers claim that 32,000 schools will be connected to the Internet by 2003, with parts of the National Curriculum taught using material accessed on-line.

The World Wide Web makes browsing on the Internet easy; each screen is called a 'page' and is like a page in a book, but can include animation as well as music.

Some useful websites are as follows:

BBC Learning Station – http://www.bbc.co.uk/education/schools
BECTa [British Educational Communications and Technology agency] – http://www.becta.org.uk (see below)
NASA – http://www.nasa.gov
Schools Net UK – http://schools.sys.uea.ac.uk/schoolnet
Schools on Line – http://www.ultralab.anglia.ac.uk/pages
Times Educational Supplement – http://www.tes.co.uk
UK Net Year – http://www.uk.net year.org
Virtual Library: Museums – http://www.musemus.reading.ac.uk/vlmp
Windows on the World – http://www.wotw.org.uk

Interactive television programmes are being piloted by the BBC, Anglia Multi-media and Granada Media and will cover courses in history, science and mathematics, reaching 30 schools. They are being linked to Internet sites, allowing teachers and students to interrupt their viewing to gather specific additional details or background information, and this video and audio material can be downloaded.

E-mail is the Internet's version of the postal service.

Tony Hannan writing in the *Oxford Magazine* (vol. 12, issue no. 1, Michaelmas, 1999) commented:

> In the next 50 years we're looking at new technology which we can't even imagine now coming into play … we're still limited by the computational power of computers. The way the brain computes has virtually no similarity with computers, though it makes some pretty tough computational choices.

BECTa and other companies offer a managed service with an integrated package of equipment, facilities and services, with clear points of contact for support and advice. BECTa, Milburn Hill Road, Science Park, Coventry CV4 7JJ. Tel: 01203 416994. (The journal *MAPE* is published in association with BECTa.)

MAPE Publications, 121 Fitzroy Avenue, Harborne, Birmingham B17 8RG.

Department for Education and Employment – www.dfee.gov.uk

Virtual Teacher Centre – http://vtc.ngfl.gov.uk

Austin, R. (1995) 'Computer conferencing in history: studying the past with the technology of the future'. *HA*.
Campbell, R. and Davies, I. 'Information highway'. *TH*, **88**, July, 33–6.
Curtis, S. (1994) 'Communication in history'. *TH*, **77**, October, 25–9.
De Cicco, E., Farmer, E. and Hargrave, M. (1998) *Using the Internet in Secondary Schools*. London: Kogan Page.
Denley, P., Fogelvik, S. and Harvey, C. (1989) *History and Computing*. Manchester: Manchester University Press.

Francis, J. (1983) *Microcomputers and Teaching History*. Harlow: Longman.
Ibbitson, M. (1990) 'GCSE history computer aided course work'. *TH*, **58**, January, 27–30.

Institute of Historical Research.   The Institute has been the University of London's centre for advanced study in history since 1921. An important resource and meeting place, it contains an open-access library, a common room and a computer training room. It publishes works of reference, administers a number of research projects and runs courses and conferences. It offers research fellowships and other awards and is part of London University's School of Advanced Study, giving opportunities for advanced national and international research. It is situated at Senate House, Malet Street, London WC1E 7HU. Tel: 0207 862 8740; fax: 0207 436 2193; e-mail: ihr@sas.ac.uk; website: http://www.ihrinfo.ac.uk; tel net: tel net.ihrinfo.ac.uk

Ireland.   Ireland's history cannot be summarized briefly. Strands of political, religious and economic problems run very deep throughout the complicated story of the country. Unlike many other comparable histories, a balanced interpretation of the known history is extremely hard to achieve; fact becomes mixed with prejudice and myth. And yet some attempt must be made to understand the relationship between Eire and Ulster. This involves, and at the same time, the emotional connections with the USA and the political position of Ulster within the United Kingdom. Three approaches to the teaching of Ireland are suggested.

In many ways the most traditional approach is to trace the history of Ireland through its leaders: Grattan, Wolfe Tone, Parnell, Collins, De Valera. Most of the prominent personalities in Irish history had fascinating lives and provide an intriguing context for the struggles in which they were engaged.

Another approach is through religion, in particular the differences in the attitudes between Protestants and Catholics. These differences are not only spiritual, but involve a whole way of life. Using this approach might offer an opportunity for collaboration with the religious education teacher.

Irish culture is colourful, emotional and very beautiful. *Riverdance* has aroused much interest; other rich fields include Irish literature and pop music.

Hogan, G. (1995) *Ireland and the European Union*. London: Sweet & Maxwell.
Hutton, S. and Stewart, P. (1991) *Ireland's Histories*. London: Routledge.

Islam.   The second largest religion after Christianity, having at least 1000 million adherents. It is a complete way of life, governing every conceivable aspect. There are 45 nations in the world where Muslims form the majority, and in most of these the majority is an over-whelming one.

All that is required for conversion to Islam is to recite two phrases: 'There is no God but Allah' and 'Mohammed is the messenger of Allah', and to accept the obligations of Islamic law.

Islam, translated from the Arabic, means submission or obedience to the will and laws of Allah as set down in the Koran. The word Muslim means 'that person or thing which obeys Allah's law'.

For Muslims there is only one merciful, eternal and all-powerful Allah. He has revealed his truths through a series of prophets, starting with Adam and ending with Mohammed. Mohammed was born not later than 570 AD and his father was Abdullah, Servant of God. He was poor and something of an outcast. He believed himself to be Shiloh, the first and last non-Jewish Prophet. From his early twenties he began to have religious experiences and visions; his first revelation came in 610 AD during a period of solitary meditation on Mount Jabal Nur near Mecca. The Archangel Gabriel told him: 'Recite in the name of your Lord.' It is believed Mohammed spoke the actual words of Allah. In the 23 remaining years of his life he had 114 separate revelations which were compiled into the Koran (Qur'an), the Arabic for recitation.

Islam is a powerful force in the world. Students need to understand the role of the religion historically, in the struggle for independence in India, in the Middle East during the foundation of Israel, in the international conflicts with the oil-producing countries, and in the fast-growing number of believers. Students should also understand the strictness of Islam's requirements. It is always helpful to listen to one of its followers describe what the religion means on a day-to-day basis.

Dawood, N, J. (trans.) *The Koran.* (1976) Harmondsworth: Penguin.
Horrie, C. and Chippindale, P. (1993) *What is Islam?* London: Virgin.
Lewis, P. (1994) *Islamic Britain.* London: Tauris.
Martin, P. and R. (1994) *The Islamic World.* Cambridge: CUP (part of the Cambridge History Programme).

J

jokes. These have a place in the teaching of history: some of those jokes in *1066 and All That* have become time-honoured; others, less well-known, have a place. 'Though Waterloo was won on the playing fields of Eton, the next war will be photographed, and lost, by Cecil Beaton (Noel Coward).' Henry Ford, reported 'History is more or less bunk' in the *Chicago Tribune* of 25 May 1916.

The problem with using jokes is that the history teacher is remembered for the jokes more than the historical material they are designed to illustrate; so it is important that jokes are not used too often. Jokes should punctuate a lesson with good humour, not diminish the learning experience.

Harburg, E. Y. (1976) *History Lesson*. London.
Sellar, W. C. and Yeatman, R. J. (1930) *1066 and All That*. London: Methuen.

Judaism. Judaism is the religion of the Jews, who believe in one God, and is based on Mosaic and rabbinical teachings. It is a culture, a nation and an ethnicity, and is a historical tradition as well as a religion. 'Jewish orthodoxy is committed to practice. Piety takes the form of ritual observance rather than credal correctness.' (Anthony Quinton in the *Oxford Companion to Philosophy* (ed. Ted Honderich).

It is particularly important to try to understand the reasons why Jews were so persecuted throughout history, and especially the Holocaust. Judaism is the main religion in the state of Israel which was founded in 1948 and which has been at the centre of political turmoil since its creation. But Jews outside Israel far exceed those within Israel.

Jews have been successful throughout the world – in finance, business and the arts. For many who practise their religion, as well as those who do not, family life is central.

See separate entry on **Holocaust.**

Baeck, L. (1961) *The Essence of Judaism.* New York: Schocken.
Kaploun, U. (1973) *The Synagogue.* Jerusalem: Keter.

K

Key Skills. *See **General National Vocational Qualification***.

Keynes. John Maynard Keynes (1883–1946) believed that the effects of an erratic trade cycle could be reduced if governments raise taxes in times of prosperity and increase spending in times of recession. Marx had predicted that this cycle of 'boom and slump' would ultimately lead to the collapse of capitalism, and so the economic ideas of Keynes provided an alternative to that offered by Marx.

Keynes played a major role in the Bretton Woods Conference in 1944, which led to the establishment of the International Monetary Fund and the World Bank. He believed that his contribution to the international monetary system was the practical expression of his belief in controlling the trade cycle.

This approach to economics has been widely adopted in the present century and is associated with many crises and other events such as the Depression, the Wall Street crash of 1929, the removal of Britain from the Gold Standard and the foundation of the Labour government after the Second World War.

Monetarism represented an opposite view to that of Keynes. The leading protagonist was Milton Friedman, and Margaret Thatcher and Augusto Pinochet were two of its leading exponents. Monetarism is the belief that governments should concentrate on achieving stability of prices through managing the money supply.

An advanced class, preferably in association with an economist, could examine whether the ideas of Keynes, are reflected in the economic conduct of governments in the free world. Totalitarian governments, such as those of Nazi Germany or the Communist USSR, do not contain the essential flexibility to operate Keynesian economic policy or monetarism. A useful study for older students would be to analyse the nature of the economic policies of successive

British governments since the war. This would involve the study of events in British history during that period.

Davies, J. B. (1995) *Keynes' Philosophical Development*. Cambridge: CUP.

Keynes, J. M. (1919) *Economic Consequences of the Peace*.

Keynes, J. M. (1936) *General Theory of Employment, Interest and Money*.

Keynes, J. M. (1936) *Treatise on Money*.

L

Labour Party. The Labour Party was formally created in 1906, formed a minority government in 1924 and has been either the party of government or opposition ever since. To understand the Labour Party it is necessary to appreciate the fundamental links with the trade unions; the association, from time to time, with the Liberals; the nature of Clause Four in their constitution, which committed Labour to the common ownership of industry; and the embracing of nationalization and the Welfare State. All these have figured prominently in the fortunes of the party in the past. Currently, Tony Blair is seeking to find a 'middle way' for the Labour Party in British politics, which seeks to espouse policies like the combination of public and private funding in industry, the latter of which had previously been associated with the Conservative Party.

For the teacher, the teaching of the history of any political party is fraught with the danger that prejudice, for or against that party, might be unintentionally expressed. A time-honoured solution in many schools is to hold a mock election – local or general – in which the sharpest political view can be expressed, but not attributed to the teacher. The teacher's role would be as a neutral chairman or returning officer. Many students enjoy greatly mock elections and, if they are carefully staged and the current manifestos from the parties have been obtained and explained, they can be of considerable benefit. What has always been dangerous is to invite the real candidates in an election to speak in a school. There is no doubt that the headteacher should be fully consulted; the history teacher also must decide if the proposal is wise.

Reekes, A. (1991) *The Rise of Labour.* London: Macmillan.

legislation and education reports (relating to history).
1971 Schools Council 8–13 Project (Place, Home and Society for history, geography, social sciences)
1972 Schools Council History Project 13–16
1985 History in the Primary and Secondary Years (An HMI view)
1988 Education Reform Act (This provided for the establishment of the National Curriculum)
1988 History from 5–16 (HMSO)
1989 History Working Group (National Curriculum Final Report)
1990 History from 5–16 (HMSO)
1991 History in the National Curriculum (the Statutory Order)
1991 History and Geography at KS4 (NCC)
1991 History, non-Statutory Guidance (NCC)
1992 Teaching History KS3 (NCC)
1993 Teaching History KS1 (SEAC)
1993 Teaching History KS2 (NCC)
1993 History Pupils' Work Assessed (SEAC for COI)
1993 OFSTED Implementations of the Curriculum Requirements of the Education Reform Act
1994 OFSTED Review of Inspection Findings from the Office of HM Chief Inspector of Schools
1995 Education (National Curriculum) (Attainment targets and programmes of study in history)
1996 Education Act 1996 (repeals Acts of 1944, 1946, 1948, 1953, 1959, 1961, 1964, 1970, 1975, 1976, 1979, 1981, 1984, 1993. The Acts of 1980, 1986 and 1988 were substantially but not wholly repealed by the 1996 Act.)

letters. These, as well as speeches, dispatches and signals, are the evidence of past events. The significance of so many famous speeches or letters is that they bring immediate colour and a human touch to what might otherwise seem commonplace. Sometimes they are about famous people or events; sometimes about minor happenings. A letter from a young private soldier at the front in the 1914–18 war is as important and poignant as one from Winston Churchill to his mother while serving in the Boer War.

Occasionally, speeches have been of great significance: Disraeli in the Commons could often use language that could move the emotions of the country, even though what he said was sometimes little different to that of his rival Gladstone. The Midlothian Campaign must have been dull. The Commons has also heard memorable words from, among many, Lloyd George, Aneurin Bevan and Enoch

Powell. It has also heard wit and humour, such as the final exchange between Margaret Thatcher and Dennis Skinner.

Martin Luther King's speech at a Civil Rights march in Washington, on 28 August 1963, was memorable: 'I have a dream that my four little children will one day live in a nation where they will not be judged by the colour of their skin, but by the content of their character.' From the same country comes equally powerful speeches throughout its history. One of these came from President Kennedy, on 1 February 1961: 'Let us negotiate out of fear. But let us never fear to negotiate.'

Signals are a military method of communication. They are short, to the point and succinct. The Royal Navy has mastered the art of signalling and no-one did it better than Nelson, on 21 October 1805 – at the Battle of Trafalgar, a major British victory in the Napoleonic War – when he sent the message: 'England expects that every man will do his duty.'

On occasion, messages have been used for less wholesome reasons than for rallying support before a battle. The murderer Dr Crippen was targeted by Morse Code as he sailed across the Atlantic with his mistress, Ethel le Neve. As he arrived in New York the police were waiting for him.

Reuters, an agency dealing with distributing news and telegraphic messages, was founded in 1859, and soon afterwards, racing news was being relayed from Newmarket. In 1870 the telegraph was taken into the Post Office. As a result, news, including up-to-the-minute speeches, were being relayed around the world, and short personal telegrams, at home, began to replace letters and cards. Eventually, much of this kind of communication, particularly in business, was achieved by telex, then fax, then e-mail. Whatever the medium, the message remains the same, and it is the message, whether given by flags, Morse Code or the computer, that can enhance a story or a narrative. As some comedians would advise: 'Never forget the one-liners!'

Collins, O. (1998) *Speeches that Changed the World: History in the Making.* London: Harper Collins.

Liberalism.   Aims to safeguard the freedom of the rational individual in society. Freedom of choice will be possible if there are genuine options from which to choose, although real choices are sometimes dependent on economic or geographical circumstances.

In about 1830, Liberalism became associated with a *laissez-faire* philosophy which advocated a non-interventionist approach and was thus in direct contrast to collectivism. *Laissez-faire* attitudes were accepted by the expanding nineteenth-century business economy and the industrial community because it allowed them so much freedom. For these reasons some critics of Liberalism felt it was a glorification of self-interest and of certain aspects of capitalism. Friction between Liberalism and community interest was one of the philosophical questions discussed by J. S. **Mill**. He believed that truth emerged from free debate rather than from coercion or paternalism, yet he admitted that Liberalism was only viable in countries that shared a sense of common nationhood.

The connections between nineteenth-century Liberalism, including the Gladstonian emphasis on individualism, and modern liberal thinking are tenuous. Harold Laski, of the London School of Economics, considers that Liberalism had exhausted itself in forlorn attempts to copy Socialism. Such a cynical view does not encompass the much later moves by the Liberal Party to arrange easy, and uneasy, relationships with the Labour Party. Nowadays, Liberals see the state as a valuable protector of human rights and therefore place a bigger emphasis on tradition and collective interest. Cole (1995) claimed that 'The primacy of basic rights is endorsed by an unbroken line of Liberals.'

A useful approach to teaching the importance of individual rights is to demonstrate the working of proportional representation as favoured by the present-day Liberal Democratic Party.

See separate entry on **voting systems.**

Cole, M. (1995) 'Liberalism'. *MHR*, **64**, April, 23–4.
Hattersley, R. (1987) *Choose Freedom*. London: Michael Joseph.
Stevenson, J. (1993) *Third Party Politics since 1945*. Oxford: Blackwell.

libraries.   The character of a library is as important as the books it contains and is expressed in its layout, the arrangement of books, notice boards, displays, newspapers, the Local History section and the helpfulness of the staff. In some respects it could be seen as a sort of website. Modern technology, however, though complementary, is not a substitute. In a perfect world the library and the website would work in tandem.

Students should be introduced to libraries, whether in the school, college or the town. It is helpful to talk about what the library offers, conduct a visit, enrol students, guiding them through the application forms, which are sometimes forbidding and, thereafter, encourage the students to visit the library, recommend books to them and ensure that the library is mentioned in work being undertaken.

Some specialist help is also advantageous for those going on to higher education; how to use a large college library is an essential preparation for tertiary education. Many universities offer introduction library visits and these are essential.

The Copyright Act 1911 requires that 'The publisher of every book published in the United Kingdom shall, within one month after the publication, deliver, at his own expense, a copy of the book to the British Library Board.' There are six Legal Deposit Libraries: British Library, Euston Road; The Bodleian Library, Oxford; The University Library, Cambridge; The National Library of Scotland, Edinburgh; The Library, Trinity College, Dublin; and The National Library of Wales.

local history.   Local history is much more than family recollections; sometimes it is wise to start in the town where the student lives and, from that point, move on to survey the national scene.

Sources and resources are critical, and although local libraries, record offices and newspaper offices hold significant collections they all need sifting and sorting. In this field, availability is almost a handicap and the useability of the material is often enhanced if it is photocopied and put into a large envelope. This avoids the problem of having too much material available.

Relating the local to the national is generally easier than one might expect. For example, a project on John Wesley, conducted in Barnsley, and aimed at describing his work and his contribution to the changes in the Church of England, can be happily, but unexpectedly, enhanced by simply showing the stone on which he stood when making a preaching tour of Yorkshire. Alternatively the immediacy of the Spanish Armada can be brought home to children by taking them to the Cobb in Lyme Regis from which it would have been possible to see the ships as they passed by. King Stephen leaps from the history books pages when Lincoln schoolchildren are told that he besieged their castle.

Interest in local history seems to have no age constraints and it is pleasing to know that many students whose interest is fired at school retain that interest throughout their lives.

British Association for Local History, 25 Lower Street, Harnham, Salisbury, Wilts. Tel: 01722 332158; fax: 01722 413242.

Family Records Centre, 1 Myddleton Street, London EC1R 1VW.

The Local Historian, 7 Carisbrooke Park, Leicester. Tel: 0116 270 5028.

Collicott, S. (1993) 'A way of looking at history'. *TH*, **72**, July, 18–23.
Duffy, T. (1986) 'Developing a skills-based approach in teaching local history', *TH*, **44**, February, 20–2.
Graham, E. J. (1988) 'Local history studies in the classroom', *TH*, **53**, October.
Hey, D. (1997) 'Sources for local history since 1800', *MHR*, **9**(2), November, 22–3.
Woodward, D. (1995) 'Sources and methods in local history', *TH*, **80**, June, 33–5.

Luther.   Martin Luther (1483–1546) was a German theologian from Wittenberg; an Augustinian friar, a priest, a professor of biblical theology and one of the leaders of the Protestant Reformation. He believed salvation was a divine gift of grace and revelation, and that God shows his intentions through scripture. He believed in justification by faith alone and challenged the hierarchy of the Catholic Church to debate issues such as the role of the papacy, the priesthood and the necessity of certain sacraments and observances. He attacked the sale of indulgences and fastened 95 'theses', essential theological statements, to the door of the church at Wittenberg on 31 October 1517. He defended his reforming doctrines before Charles V, the Holy Roman Emperor, but was nevertheless excommunicated from the Church of Rome. He never sought a break from Rome but felt that the Church put him in an impossible position. As a result other Protestants accepted his views and alternative churches to the Church of Rome were founded. Luther ended up being 'protected' by Elector Frederich of Saxony, married Katherine von Bora in 1525 and fathered six children.

He is included in this book because, with **Calvin** and **Zwingli**, he spearheaded the Protestant movement which

> Propagated their views across Europe in an unstoppable flood. For practical purposes, the main division lay between the so-called 'Magisterial Protestants', like Luther and Calvin, who sought to replace the state backed monopoly of the Catholic Church with similar monopolies of their own, and the so-called 'Radical Protestants', such as the Anabaptists and anti-Trinitarians who professed every sort of extreme idea from pacifism to democratic congregationalism and, most dangerously, religious tolerance. (Norman Davies (1999) *The History of the Isles*. London: Macmillan. Serialized in *The Times*, 3 November 1999, p. 45.)

Much modern Protestant theology still derives from much that Luther pinned to the Wittenberg church door. Present-day evangelists have employed various techniques and presentational mechanisms but their essential spiritual teaching is founded in the sixteenth century. To ignore Luther and his influences in modern Europe is to give an unbalanced appreciation of continental development.

website: Martin Luther – http://www.geocities.com/vienna/1667/Luther.htm

M

Machiavelli. Niccolo Machiavelli (1469–1527) wrote *The Prince* in 1513. It was a book of advice to monarchs on the best means to acquire and retain power. Some cynics have claimed that successful politicians have been influenced by it ever since. It was written after he had lost power in Florence following the restoration of the Medicis in 1512. He had been secretary to the Republic of Florence but never returned to power again even after the Medicis had fallen in 1527.

He believed a strong state was necessary in order to achieve all other human ends and he stressed the need for a vigorous code of morality to preserve the public spirit of the citizens. This is often simplified to 'The end justifies the means'. What Machiavelli is advocating is the need to appear to be a strong, autocratic ruler whose task is to work on behalf of the people he serves. *The Prince* is a seminal book and one of the most telling and influential of political texts.

Students find it easy to accept or reject what Machiavelli stood for – it is a clear, strident philosophy – and his life in Florence enhances greatly his appeal. Time, as well as modern political developments, has not diminished his influence. It would be worthwhile to consider the relevance of his writing to the subject of the possession of political power nowadays, and how it is acquired and retained. It was Francis Bacon, in *The Advancement of Learning*, who wrote, 'We are much beholden of Machiavelli and others, that write what men do, and not what they ought to do.'

See separate entry on the **Renaissance**.

Curry, P. and Zarate, O. (1990) Machiavelli Audiotape (featuring Derek Jacobi). Icon Audio (approx. duration: 2 hours).

Magna Carta. The Magna Carta, or Great Charter, was signed by King John at Runnymede on 15 June 1215. Four copies in Latin currently exist on single-skin vellum. They measure 14 in. x 17 ½ in. and contain 76 lines. Two copies are in the British Library, one is in Salisbury and one in Lincoln.

The essence of the Charter can be expressed in three clauses. One says that 'No free man shall be taken or imprisoned or disseised or outlawed or exiled or in any way ruined, nor will we go or send against him, except by the lawful judgement of his peers or by the law of the land.' The second says that 'No one will we sell, to no one will we deny or delay right of justice.' The third says: 'All these aforesaid customs and liberties, the observance of which we have granted in our Kingdom as far as pertains to us towards our men, shall be observed by all in our Kingdom, as well clergy as laymen, as far as pertains to them towards their men.' As Sir Edward Coke (1532–1634), the MP for Buckingham, said in the Lords' Amendment to the Petition of Right, on 17 May 1629, in speaking against illegal imprisonment, 'Magna Carta is such a fellow, that he will have no Sovereign.'

Britain does not have a written constitution, but has a partly written one, and the Magna Carta is intrinsic to what we have. It is ponderous, legalistic and rather dull, but it is also part of our essential national character. It is quietly explosive and represents a bulwark and defence against oppression. It was a successful attempt to create a free, independent, protective state.

Dickinson, J. C. (1955) 'The great charter: a translation'. HA General Series, **31**.
Hindley, G. (1990) *The Book of the Magna Carta*. London: Constable.
Holt, J. C. (1992) *Magna Carta* (Seminar Studies in History). Cambridge: CUP.
Jones, J. A. P. (1971) *King John and the Magna Carta*. Harlow: Longman.
Stroud, D. I. (1998) *Magna Carta*. Southampton: Paul Care Publications.

Mao and Maoism. Maoism was the distinctive communist philosophy of Mao Tse Tung (Mao Zedong) (1893–1976). It was distinctive because he placed the emphasis for revolutionary advance with the rural peasantry rather than with the urban proletariat, as in the Soviet Union. He believed in the idea of permanent revolution expressed in radical reform; an attempt to galvanize economic and political development and a dramatic attempt to radicalize the country and prevent the revolution from stagnating. He advocated agricultural collectivization and included in that the drafting of city workers and intellectuals from the cities to the country. Most of these policies proved economically and socially disastrous and have been largely reversed. But Maoist revolutionary theory and strategies for guerilla warfare are still adopted in some developing countries and in less developed ones also. Mao had developed these in the long war with the Kuomintang after it had turned on its communist allies in 1927. His Long March (1934–5) caused him to create a new base in north-west China and it established his credibility with the peasantry as their leader and with China as a whole as a major force with which to be reckoned. With Zhu De and Lin Biao he was able to resist the Japanese and to defeat Chiang Kai-shek, and on 1 October 1949 he proclaimed the People's Republic of China.

Many students are interested in the mystique of Mao. Like **Gandhi** he lived simply, dressed traditionally and represented a total contrast to imperial China. He had ideological differences with the Soviet Union, and this is a helpful distinction because it makes the crucial point that communism comes in various forms. Though Marx is the midwife, the children differ greatly; Maoism is one of those distinctive children.

However, students are also interested in the massive changes that took place. The Long March was a force of 10,000 evacuated from south-eastern China because the Kuomintang army was attacking and they marched to north-western China. Mao took over the leadership and for nine months travelled through mountains and across rivers. Eventually 6000 survivors, having marched 6000 miles, reached Yan'an. It established Mao as an effective leader beyond all doubt. The Great Leap Forward (1958) was a comparable brave attempt at economic and political development. The Cultural Revolution (1966) was a very dramatic attempt to push the revolution on further. All these major innovations are colourful, exciting developments and capture the imagination.

Shool, P. (1999) *Mao*. London: Hodder and Stoughton.

maps.   Maps are indispensable to the understanding of history. It is impossible to follow a military campaign without them. They show graphically the growth of towns, and they give a unique perspective to a county, a country, a continent and to the world, which economic or political considerations don't always provide.

Sketch-maps are particularly helpful in emphasizing geographical features, or the essential elements of a location, where a printed map might confuse by too much detail. The immediacy of a sketch can give momentum to a lesson. Once the art is learned, the value to students in answering examination questions is considerable.

For some work in history, a relief map is particularly advantageous. For example, the geographical location of Stalingrad and the relationship between the city and the river are important to an appreciation of the Siege. Another example can be seen in the unification of Italy, where political differences arose, in part, out of the nature of the terrain – mountains, sea and rivers. These physical features had been the reason why some small states had existed in the first place and resulted in a separateness which overrode many political arguments.

Maps used in class teaching must be up to date. To look at a 1950s map of Africa is to look at a different continent from that which exists nowadays. Although most of the political boundaries are the same, the names have completely changed. Many of the implicit differences, like the changes from a colonial to an independent state, are obvious.

Modern maps can also portray many socio-economic statistics. It is helpful to see the national or continental distribution of population, or the particular prevalence of diseases. It is now commonplace for newspapers to express the national distribution of party-political affiliations in map form.

Boys, A. (1998) *An Atlas of World Affairs*. London: Routledge.
Mills, D. (ed.) (1988) *Geographical Work in Primary and Secondary Schools*. Sheffield: Geographical Association.
Smith, D. (1982) *Antique Maps of the British Isles*. London: Batsford.

Marx.   Karl Heinrich Marx (1818–83) was the son of a Jewish lawyer and married a rabbi's daughter. He studied at Bonn and Berlin, completed his degree at 23 (in 1841) and edited many radical publications in Belgium, Rhineland and France between 1842 and 1848. His philosophy of historical materialism strides the twentieth century like a colossus, either because his beliefs are followed slavishly or because they are so vehemently opposed. He is considered the scourge of capitalism, the prophet of the working-classes and a guru in the eyes of many students. To teach his philosophy is difficult because much of it is so opaque.

He was introduced to the working-class movement in Paris in 1844. He worked with Friedrich Engels (1820–95) and produced with him the Communist Manifesto (1848), which was described by the twentieth-century English historian David Thomson as, 'beyond doubt one of the most important documents of modern history'. It explained a programme for revolution, involving class war, world revolution and the overthrow of the existing social order. Issued in a year when Europe was in political turmoil the Manifesto was explosive.

Eventually Marx enlarged the Manifesto into a series of books, one of which was *Das Kapital*, published in 1867 when we was 49 years old. Much of it is based on **Hegel**ian dialectic, and this is not surprising because Marx had been a member of the Young Hegelians at University. The philosophical structure Marx adopts is the purest Hegelian philosophy. He adds, however, major sections on the abolition of classes through the class-war conflict: this would be the true beginning of history in a society directed by human beings. He saw the task of the proletarian movement as being one of self-definition – through organization, discipline and self-criticism – and anyone who has been a member of a Marxist cell will know what that means; though totally atheistic ('Religion is the opium of the people') it has the tight structure of a monastic novitiate. Townshend (1996) defines Marxism as the 'theory and practice of the proletarian revolution', and so it has been shown to be in revolutionary outbreaks throughout the world. The book also outlines an organization of political economy based on materialistic science.

A useful way of approaching the teaching of Marxism is through biographical sources. These include the different stages in the development of his ideas – home, university, 1848 Revolution, *Das Kapital*, the links with Engels and the final years.

Berlin, I. (1982) *Karl Marx*. Oxford: OUP.
Carver, T. (1991) 'Marxist interpretation of history'. *MHR*, **2**(4), April, 14–15.
Marx, K. and Engels, F. (1967) *The Communist Manifesto* (introduction by A. J. P. Taylor). Harmondsworth: Penguin.
Townshend, J. (1996) 'Marxism'. *MHR*, **8**(1), September, 7–8.
website: Marx and Engel Archive – http://www/marx.org

medicine.   The history of medicine is the story of the slow evolution from myth and superstition to scientific research. It was a long time before people learned to treat diseases correctly. Egypt and Greece pioneered many of these advances. Aristotle considered that everything was made up of four elements – earth, air, fire and water – and that each person contained four humours: hot, cold, wet and dry. Thus fire is hot and dry. Galen added three spirits – natural, vital and animal – to the earlier elements and humours. Hippocrates issued the solemn promise, called the Hippocratic oath, which has remained the principle of medical practice: 'The doctor's first duty is to do nothing to harm his patients, then to help the sick according to their ability and judgement, never give poisons, not to tell other people what their patients had told them and to keep both themselves and their profession pure.' He thereby added an ethical dimension to medicine.

Physicians received their charter in 1518, and with it came pioneer work in anatomy, physiology, pathology, bacteria and the blood. By the nineteenth century, antiseptics were being used, and antibiotics were discovered in the twentieth century. The Hippocratic oath is still observed but can now be implemented more effectively.

The range of drugs used nowadays is enormous, and this wide range, coupled with availability, has been as significant as any medical advance, and one of the most costly.

There are many chances for the history teacher to collaborate with scientific colleagues, through joint lessons, visits or guidance on essays. The study of medicine is not always familiar to school or college science teachers, which means that historians and scientists can explore a new field together in preparing of a new course.

Some of the older teaching hospitals throughout the country have fascinating small museums displaying old medical implements.

The Wellcome Institute for the History of Medicine comprises the Library, the Academic Unit, an Exhibitions Unit and the Friends Office. Further information on: www.wellcome.ac.uk/institute

Bynum, W. F. and Porter, R. (eds) (1994) *Encyclopedia of the History of Medicine*. London: Routledge.

Dawson, I. and Coulson, S. (1996) *Medicine and Health Through Time*. London: John Murray.

memorization. It is part of the learning process in history. Some are born with this gift; others have to acquire it. Sadly, memorization – learning by heart or by rote – can dominate history to the detriment of discovering a love for the subject or any of the other interests and attractions it contains. Of equal importance is the situation where memorization can become a straightjacket which inhibits or even prevents free-ranging interpretation; the blind alley that comes from thinking that knowing the facts about a historical incident is all that is required. If one compares learning the facts in history to an actor learning his lines, it is important to reach the stage where the grasp of the material is so secure that it can be interpreted sensitively.

Memorization has to be accurate or else it is dangerous. There is a cruel story from the theatre in which the actress Claudette Colbert was having difficulty remembering her part, and said to Noel Coward, 'I knew these lines backwards last night', to which Noel Coward replied, 'And that is just the way you are saying them this morning.'

Memorization does improve with practice; the more the memory is used the better it becomes. The key issue is to decide what should be learned by heart and how best to do it. Dates, spellings, sequences of events *do* matter and, when they have been thoroughly checked, can be committed to memory. This is an old-fashioned strategy, but it works if the student knows that part of the history lesson will include memory work. For older students this can consist of significant stages in a major event such as the **French Revolution**. For younger people it might be enough to learn the correct spelling of words like 'parliament', or 'sovereign', or 'villein'.

mercantilism. Prevalent in the sixteenth and seventeenth centuries, it stressed the great value of external trade and sought to limit imports. The possession of gold was all-important, and if it was not naturally present it was to be obtained by commerce. Wealth was dependent on the balance of trade, and tariffs were imposed when necessary. The Navigation Acts of 1651, 1660, 1662 and 1663 were an example of mercantilism and sought to protect the trade between England and the American colonies from external interference. The Acts were rigorously enforced by the Royal Navy and only repealed in 1849.

Supporters of free trade, like Adam **Smith**, believed that mercantilism served only the interests of the merchants and not the community as a whole.

Free trade eventually replaced mercantilism, though in a modified form, because completely free trade was impossible to achieve.

There are at least two ways of dealing with mercantilism: the first is to have a debate with one group representing its advocates and the other side its detractors. The second approach is to act out the sharply contrasted views of the British government and the American colonies concerning the Navigation Acts. It was the strict enforcement of the Navigation Acts which aroused deep resentment against the British and led to the Revolutionary War. As John Adams was able to distinguish, 'The revolution was in the minds of the people, and the union of the colonies, both of which were accomplished before hostilities commenced.'

The revolution and union were gradually forming in the years from 1760 to 1776.

See separate entry on **drama**.

Mill, John Stuart.   John Stuart Mill (1806–73) developed many of the ideas of his father James as well as those of Jeremy Bentham. They all believed in utilitarianism, which proposed that society should be organized for the greatest happiness of the greatest number. Unlike his father, however, he thought that there were different degrees of happiness and that the pleasure of serving society was of more social value, or utility, than the pleasure of caring for oneself. For most of his life he was a civil servant in the India Office, and for a short time was Radical MP for Westminster (1865–8). Utilitarianism was a controversial philosophy. For example, Charles Dickens (1812–70), in chapter two of *Hard Times*, mocks Thomas Gradgrind as a misguided utilitarian.

Mill wrote on a wide variety of subjects. His essay 'On Liberty', written in 1859, was followed by others on the extension of the franchise, proportional representation and wider factory management. The book he wrote jointly with his wife Harriet Taylor in 1869, *The Subjection of Women*, made a powerful case for the emancipation of women: 'The principle which regulates the existing social relations between the sexes – the legal subordination of one sex to the other – is wrong in itself, and now one of the chief hindrances to human improvement.'

Most of his ideas are now commonly accepted. A list of the causes he espoused reads like a list of the best of the radical reforms of the nineteenth century. Commentaries on the century are rightly concerned with the pain and dysfunction which accompanied much of the economic expansion. Mill shows that there were those living at the time who were able to see visions of the critical changes that were required. In choosing biographies which would be profitable to study in some depth, it would be appropriate to include John Stuart Mill's for the variety, originality and idealistic nature of his ideas. The relevance of his writing on the emancipation of women, the advanced nature of his ideas on voting systems and his plans for worker participation are as topical today as they were in his own day.

Cockshort, A. O. (ed.) (1992) *The Autobiography of John Stuart Mill.* Halifax: Ryburn.

mixed-ability teaching.   Finding a teaching formula which makes it possible to help children with differing abilities to learn together. It seeks to combine the academic and the social. In his book *Towards a Theory of Instruction* (1966), J. S. Bruner wrote: 'We teach a subject not to produce little living libraries on that subject, but rather to get a student ... to consider matters as an historian does, to take part in the process of knowledge getting. Knowing is a process, not a product.' By that token all students can share in the process of knowledge getting. B. L. Cooke, in chapter 5 of E. C. Wragg's book *Teaching Mixed-ability Groups* (1976) tries to move the debate forward:

> We are slowly, very slowly, coming to accept that if history in schools is to have any meaning to our pupils ... it must involve them actively ... to participate in decisions about what they study and how to do it, in searching for evidence and in asking questions of it; in reconstructing past events, incidents, developments and lives; in puzzling out problems; in putting their own findings and views in various ways ... [these] skills of inquiry, recording and expression, awareness of themselves, and awareness of the society in which they live, and its evolution. These should be denied no child, whatever his ability and however he is grouped with his fellows.

Unlike **differentiation**, mixed-ability teaching does not necessarily separate pupils. Worksheets can provide a basis for independent study, if there are adequate resources, clear referencing and a group of children who have been prepared properly in the specific techniques required for this kind of work. Drama should be included, especially for children for whom books and words are sometimes an obstacle. Modelling can also release talents and skills. In both drama and modelling, once an interest has been aroused an investigation into printed material may develop.

In mixed-ability teaching, class control can be a problem as pupils move around the classroom freely, looking for information.

They will all work at different speeds and a sensitive approach is required in guiding, managing and directing the children.

See separate entry under **differentiation**.

Davies, B. and Cave, R. (1977) *Mixed Ability Teaching in the Secondary School*. London: Ward Lock.

Johnson, S. (1979) 'An investigation into effectiveness ... of teaching history using mixed-ability groups'. BPhil thesis, Exeter University School of Education.

monasteries and monasticism.   Monasticism is the withdrawal of men and women from secular society in order to devote themselves to the religious life. The collective noun for monks, nuns and friars is 'Religious'. They take vows of poverty, chastity and obedience. They live in community, spending their time either in prayer and worship, interspersed with physical work in the monastery or in the adjacent grounds, or in the outside world, running parishes or performing pastoral duties such as work in schools, prisons or as missionaries. The major orders are Benedictine, Cistercian, Dominican, Franciscan, Augustinian and Trappist, but there are many minor orders also.

Religious have great appeal for students because their lives differ so markedly from their own. The best introduction is to visit a religious house and to witness at first hand the occupants' measured life style.

Many students enjoy making models of monasteries and there are kits, designs, scale drawings and suitable books available for guidance. It is also worthwhile inviting a monk or a nun to speak to the class.

The Dissolution of the Monasteries by Henry VIII had a profound impact on the monastic world. More recently, numbers of Religious have declined further. Many of them follow the same rules which were set in medieval times.

multi-ethnic societies.   These present challenges for the historian, especially those countries that resist them. The white Australian policy, the expulsion of Asians from Uganda or the removal of Moslems from Kosovo were attempts to prevent the creation of a multi-ethnic society. There are four contexts which are worth investigating:

Multi-ethnicity is more usually apparent in a city or town, for example, the Bangladeshi community in the east end of London, the Hindus in parts of Birmingham or the Catholic community in Liverpool.

Multi-ethnicity can also be seen in Brazil, which is a conglomerate of ethnic difference, or the USA, which, though welcoming people from all over the world, is selective as to who can live there permanently.

The Commonwealth is an expression of multi-ethnicity. It is an association of states which includes a quarter of the world's population and land surface. The 54 members cover all continents. The Commonwealth provides a network of co-operation and dialogue between countries that include most of the world's ethnic groups.

Multi-ethnicity should be included in a syllabus. Rex Walford, a geographer, and Christine Counsell, a historian, both from the Cambridge University School of Education, in a letter to *The Times* (2 February 1999) wrote:

> Giving all young people a thorough and enlightened understanding of our nation's multicultural past and of the diversity of the world's peoples is surely the basis of future racial harmony in Britain. Our best history and geography teachers foster wide knowledge of these issues and critical engagement with them. If the Secretary of State for Education would give as much attention to the teaching of geography and history as he does to so-called 'core' subjects ... much could be achieved in advancing both relevant knowledge and positive attitudes in multicultural Britain.

For students, the teaching of history can help remove dangerous myths and misconceptions regarding cultural and religious diversity and yet the teacher must always be aware that poor teaching can actually increase prejudice.

Commonwealth Institute, Kensington High Street, London W8 6NQ. Tel: 0207 603 4535; fax: 0207 602 7374; e-mail: info@commonwealth.org.uk; website: http://www.commonwealth.org.uk

Dyer, M. (1982) 'History in a multicultural society'. *HA*.
Goulbourne, H. (1998) *Race Relations in Britain since 1945*. Basingstoke: Macmillan.
Hulmes, E. (1989) *Education and Cultural Diversity*. London: Longman.
Modgil, S., Verma, G., Mellick, K., Modgil, C. (1986) *Multicultural Education: An Interminable Debate*. Brighton: Falmer.
O'Connor, E. and James, R. (1978) 'Teaching history in a multicultural society: trends in education'. London: Department of Education and Science.

museums. Museums preserve the past, protect the present and enhance the future. Over the last twenty years there has been a revolution in how museums conduct their activities. At the same time there has been an internal conflict raging between those who want to display existing material more effectively and those who believe that a modern reconstruction based on the remnants of the past is needed.

The Museums Association, at their AGM in September 1998, agreed on a definition: 'Museums enable people to explore collections for inspiration, learning and enjoyment. They are institutions that collect, safeguard and make accessible artefacts and specimens, which they hold in trust for society.'

The Museums Association organizes an annual conference, a trade fair, a number of seminars and road shows, which are regional events for anyone with a professional interest in museum issues. The Association publishes a journal, *Museum Practice*, which is the leading international guide to the care, presentation and interpretation of collections in museums and galleries; a *Museums Yearbook*, which is a directory of 3000 museums, galleries, heritage centres and historic houses in the UK and Ireland; and issues Museum Briefings, which are information sheets for general use in everyday work, presenting complex issues and legislation in a simple reference format.

Education features in the Code of Ethics (1999) of the Association: 'Museums have an educational role in the widest sense and the governing body should ensure that the museum service provides educational facilities for a broad range of interest levels and abilities.'

Teachers should aim to establish a relationship with museum staff, appreciate precisely what the museum can offer, establish which artefacts students should study, and accept the necessity of a time limit for any one visit.

Group for Education in Museums, Royal Albert Museum, Queen Street, Exeter, Devon EX4 3RX. Tel: 01392 265858; fax: 01392 421252; e-mail: membership@gem.org.uk

See separate entry on the **museums (London)***.*

Museums Association, 42 Clerkenwell Close, London EC1R OPA. Tel: 0207 608 2933; fax: 0207 250 1929.

Batto, G. R. (ed.) (1994) 'School museums and primary history'. *HA*.
Davies, M. 'Museum education and history in the National Curriculum'. *Primary Teaching Studies*, **6**(3 & 4), 216–20.
DfEE (1992) *A Survey of the Use of Artefacts and Museum Resources in Teaching National Curriculum History*. HMI Report 366/9. London: Department for Education and Employment.
Rebetz, P. (1970) *How to Visit a Museum*. Strasbourg: Council for Cultural Co-operation.

museums (London).   Bank of England, Threadneedle Street, London EC2R 8AH. Tel: 0207 601 4444.

British Library, 96 Euston Road, London NW1 2DB. Tel: 0207 412 7111; fax: 01937 546333.

British Museum (see separate entry)

Commonwealth Institute, Kensington High Street, London W8 6NO. Tel: 0207 603 4535; fax: 0207 602 7374; e-mail: info@commonwealth.org.uk; website: http://www.commonwealth.org.uk

Imperial War Museum, London SE1. Tel: 0207 416 5000; fax: 0207 416 5374; website: www.iwm.org.uk.

Museum of Childhood, Cambridge Heath Road, Bethnal Green, London E2. Tel: 0208 983 5200; fax: 0208 983 5225.

Museum of London, London Wall, London EC2Y 5HN. Tel: 0207 600 3644; fax: 0207 600 1058.

Museum of Mankind (ethnography department of the British Museum), 6 Burlington Gardens, London W1X 2EX. Tel: 0207 323 8043; fax: 0207 323 8013.

Museum of the Moving Image, South Bank, London SE1 8XT. Tel: 0207 928 3535; fax: 0207 815 1419.

National Maritime Museum, Greenwich, London SE10 9NF. Tel: 0208 858 4422; fax: 0208 312 6632.

National Gallery, Trafalgar Square, London WC2N 5DN. Tel: 0207 839 3321; fax: 0207 930 4764.

Natural History Museum, Cromwell Road, London, SW7 5BD (see entry on **science**). Tel: 0207 038 9123; fax: 0207 938 9290.

Science Museum, Exhibition Road, London SW7 2DD (see entry on **science**). Tel: 0207 938 8000; 0207 938 8080/8008 (information); fax: 0207 938 9790; website: http://www.nmsi.ac.uk

Tate Gallery, Millbank, London SW1P 4RG (also branches in Liverpool and St Ives). Tel: 0207 887 8000; fax: 0207 887 8007.

Theatre Museum, National Museum of Performing Arts, 1E Tavistock Street, London WC2E 7PA. Tel: 0207 836 7891; fax: 0207 836 5148.

Victoria and Albert Museum, South Kensington, London SW7 2RL. Tel: 0207 938 8500; fax: 0207 938 8379.

Wellington Museum, Apsley House, 149 Piccadilly, London W1V 9FA. Tel: 0207 499 5676; fax: 0207 493 6576.

Adams, C. and Miller, S. (1982) 'Museums and the use of evidence in history'. *TH*, **34**(65), 28–30.
Bardwell, S. and Meek, R. (1991) 'Learning about museum resources'. *TH*, **65**, October.
Barwell, J. (1990) 'Museums and the National Curriculum'. *TH*, **61**, October, 25–31.
Fairley, J. (1977) *History Teaching Through Museums*. London: Longman.
Goalen, P. (1993) 'MOMI: the Museum of the Moving Image. *Hindsight GCSE Modern History Review*, **3**(3).
Winterbottom, N. (1986) 'The group for education in museums'. *TH*, **44**, February, 24–5.

music.   Music is part of our daily experience. It tells a story, sets a scene, provides a context, stimulates the faint-hearted and 'stirs the blood'. Historians can easily forget the significance of music in teaching; it can often enhance a lesson to play an appropriate piece of music. Whole slices of history may be introduced by, for example, the 1812 Overture of Tchaikovsky, *La Marseillaise* by Rouget de L'isle or the symphonic poem *Ma Vlast* by Smetana.

Grant, D. J. and Palisca, C. V. (1988) *A History of Western Music* (4th edn). London: Norton.
Kennedy, M. (1997) *The Oxford Dictionary of Music* (Rev. edn). Oxford: OUP.
Reed, W. L. and Bristow, M. J. (1998) *National Anthems of the World*. London: Cassell.
Simon, W. L. (ed.) (1991) *Reader's Digest Festival of Popular Songs*. London: Reader's Digest.

Napoleon (1769–1821). His achievements as a soldier, a politician and a statesman are of the highest order. Napoleon should be assessed with regard to his contribution to France. He was promoted at the of 26 and was in supreme command of the campaign against Sardinia and Austria between 1796 and 1797. He played a major part in the French Revolutionary Wars, although Nelson frustrated his plan to create an overseas empire, and also his challenge to the British overland route to India, by defeating him in the Battle of the Nile 1798.

Napoleon joined a conspiracy that overthrew the Directory, was elected First Consul and became the Supreme Ruler of France. It was at this stage that he reorganized the country through the legal system, introducing the 'Code Napoleon', and also through the general administration of France, especially in relation to the church and to education.

He crowned himself Emperor, created an Imperial Court and proceeded to restrict the more liberal provisions of the revolutionary constitution. A European coalition was formed against him which he resisted. He defeated the Austrians at Ulm, and then the combined Austrian and Russian armies at Austerlitz in 1805. But Nelson defeated him at Trafalgar in 1805. In retaliation, Napoleon introduced the Continental System, with which he attempted to stop all trade with Britain and its European allies, but this proved difficult to enforce. He led a disastrous invasion of Russia in 1812, made serious misjudgements in the Peninsular War (1807–14) and was defeated at Leipzig (1813). He abdicated in 1814 and was exiled to Elba. He soon returned, but was defeated again at Waterloo (1815) before being exiled again to St Helena. Nevertheless, his dominance in Europe had wide-reaching effects on political developments in many countries for some half a century afterwards.

It is helpful, in explaining Napoleon's life and achievements if they are structured in three stages, as above; otherwise they can become confusing. However, the diverse nature of his achievements lend themselves to what is sometimes called 'creative fragmentation'; students can create a book, with sections written separately and then joined together as a continuous narrative.

Barnett, C. (1978) *Bonaparte*. London: Allen and Unwin.
Howard, D. (ed.) (1986) *Napoleonic Military History: A Bibliography*. New York: Garland.
Pelling, J. (1978) *The Emperor Napoleon*. Cambridge: CUP.

National Curriculum. Formally introduced by Kenneth Baker, then Secretary of State for Education, in 1988. Before that, schools were free to choose whether or not they would follow any nationally devised schemes. Baker's original design is still in place but was revised in September 1995 and September 2000.

Pupils of compulsory school age in maintained schools in England are organized into four categories:

	Age	Year group
Key Stage 1	5–7	1–2
Key Stage 2	7–11	3–6
Key Stage 3	11–14	7–9
Key Stage 4	14–16	10–11

History is taught at Key Stages 1 and 2, but there is now no requirement for history to be taught at Key Stage 4 unless it is chosen as a subject for GCSE or for the Certificate of Attainment. At each stage, programmes of study are set out, and in history there is only one attainment target which sets out expected standards. Since 1995, in history, there have been eight levels described, of increasing difficulty, with an additional level above 8, to help teachers to differentiate students' performance. By the end of Key Stage 1, the performance of the great majority of pupils should be within the range of levels 1–3; by the end of Key Stage 2, it should be within the range of 2–5; and by the end of Key Stage 3, within the range of 3–7. Level 8 is for very able pupils and, to help teachers to distinguish exceptional performance at Key Stage 3, there is a level above level 8.

Programmes of Study: Common Requirements

Access. The programme of study for each Key Stage should be taught to the majority of pupils at that stage, in ways appropriate to their abilities. For the small number of pupils who need it, material may be selected from earlier or later Key Stages, where necessary, to enable pupils to progress. Such material should be presented in a manner which is suited to the pupil's age.

Appropriate provision should be made for pupils who need to use:

means of communication other than speech, including computers, technological aids, signing, symbols or lip-reading; non-sighted methods of reading, such as Braille or non-visual or non-aural ways of acquiring information; technological aids in practical and written work; and aids or adapted equipment to allow access to practical activities within and out of school.

Use of Language. Pupils should be taught to express themselves clearly both in speech and writing and to develop their reading skills. They should be taught to use grammatically correct sentences and to spell and punctuate accurately in order to communicate effectively in written English.

Information Technology. Pupils should be given opportunities, where appropriate, to develop and apply their IT capability in their study of history.

Key Elements

Chronology. Pupils should be taught:

(a) to sequence events and objects, in order to develop a sense of chronology; and

(b) to use common words and phrases relating to the passing of time, e.g. old, new, before, after, long ago, days of the week, months, years.

Range and depth of historical knowledge and understanding. Pupils should be taught:

(a) about aspects of the past through stories from different periods and cultures, including stories and eyewitness accounts of historical events;

(b) to recognize why people did things, why events happened and what happened as a result; and

(c) to identify differences between ways of life at different times.

Interpretations of history. Pupils should be taught:

(a) to identify different ways in which the past is represented, e.g. pictures, written accounts, films, television programmes, plays, songs, reproductions of objects, museum displays.

Historical enquiry. Pupils should be taught:

(a) how to find out about aspects of the past from a range of sources of information including artefacts, pictures and photographs, adults talking about their own past, written sources, buildings and sites; and

(b) to ask and answer questions about the past.

Organization and communication. Pupils should be taught:

(a) to communicate their awareness and understanding of history in a variety of ways.

Key Stage 1: Programme of Study Pupils should be given opportunities to develop an awareness of the past and of the ways it differs from the present. They should be helped to set their study of the past in a chronological framework and to understand some of the ways in which we find out about the past.

The areas of study and the key elements (outlined below) should be taught together.

Areas of Study. Pupils should be taught about the everyday life, work, leisure and culture of men, women and children in the past, e.g. clothes, diet, everyday objects, houses, shops and other buildings, jobs, transport, entertainment. In progressing from familiar situations to those more distant in time and place, pupils should be given opportunities to investigate (a) changes in their own lives and those of their family or adults around them; and (b) aspects of the way of life of people in Britain in the past, beyond living memory.

Pupils should be taught about the lives of different kinds of famous men and women, including personalities drawn from British history, e.g. rulers, saints, artists, engineers, explorers, inventors and pioneers.

Pupils should be taught about past events of different types, including events from the history of Britain, e.g. notable local and national events, events in other countries, events that have been remembered and commemorated by succeeding generations such as centenaries, religious festivals, anniversaries, the Gunpowder Plot and the Olympic Games.

Key Stage 2: Programme of Study

Study Units: Key Elements:

Study Unit 1	Romans, Anglo Saxons and Vikings in Britain
Study Unit 2	Life in Tudor Times
Study Unit 3a	Victorian Britain
Study Unit 3b	Britain Since 1930
Study Unit 4	Ancient Greece
Study Unit 5	Local History
Study Unit 6	A Past Non-European Society

Key Stage 3: Programme of Study

Study Units: Key Elements:

Study Unit 1	Medieval Realms: Britain 1066–1500
Study Unit 2	The Making of the United Kingdom: Crowns, Parliament and Peoples 1500–1750
Study Unit 3	Britain 1750 – circa 1900
Study Unit 4	The Twentieth-century World
Study Unit 5	An Era or Turning Point in European History before 1914
Study Unit 6	A Past Non-European Society

Attainment Targets: Level Descriptions. The following level descriptions describe the types and range of performance that pupils working at a particular level should characteristically demonstrate. In deciding on a pupil's level of attainment at the end of the Key Stage, teachers should judge which description best fits the pupil's performance. Each description should be considered in conjunction with the descriptions for adjacent levels.

By the end of Key Stage 1, the performance of the majority of pupils should be within the range of levels 1–3; by the end of Key Stage 2 it should be within the range 2–5; and by the end of Key Stage 3, within the range 3–7. Level 8 is available for very able pupils and, to help teachers differentiate exceptional performance at Key Stage 3, there is a level above level 8.

Level 1. Pupils recognize the distinction between present and past in their own and other people's lives. They show their emerging sense of chronology by sequencing a few events and objects and by using everyday terms to describe the passing of time. They know and can recount episodes from stories about the past. They are beginning to find answers to questions about the past from sources of information.

Level 2. Pupils show their developing sense of chronology by using terms concerned with the passing of time, by ordering events and objects and by making distinctions between aspects of their own lives and past times. They demonstrate factual knowledge and understanding of aspects of the past beyond living memory, and of some of the main events and people they have studied. They are beginning to recognize that there are reasons why people in the past acted as they did. They are beginning to identify some of the different ways in which the past is represented. They answer questions about the past, from sources of information, on the basis of simple observations.

Level 3. Pupils show their understanding of chronology through their increasing awareness that the past can be divided into different periods of time, their recognition of some of the similarities and differences between these periods and their use of dates and terms. They demonstrate factual knowledge and understanding of some of the main events, people and changes drawn from the appropriate programme of study. They are beginning to give a few reasons for, and results of, the main events and changes. They identify some of the different ways in which the past is represented. They find answers to questions about the past by using sources of information in ways that go beyond simple observations.

Level 4. Pupils demonstrate factual knowledge and understanding of aspects of the history of Britain and other countries, drawn from the Key Stage 2 or Key Stage 3 programme of study. They use this to describe the characteristic features of past societies and periods and to identify changes within and across periods. They describe some of the main events, people and changes. They give some reasons for, and results of, the main events and changes. They show how some aspects of the past have been represented and interpreted in different ways. They are beginning to select and combine information from sources. They are beginning to produce structured work, making appropriate use of dates and terms.

Level 5. Pupils demonstrate an increasing depth of factual knowledge and understanding of aspects of the history of Britain and other countries drawn from the Key Stage 2 or Key Stage 3 programmes of study. They use this to describe, and to begin to make links between, features of the past societies and periods. They describe events, people and changes. They describe, make links between and give reasons for, and results of, events and changes. They know that some events, people and changes have been interpreted in different ways and suggest possible reasons for this. Using their knowledge and understanding, pupils are beginning to evaluate sources of information and to identify those that are useful for particular tasks. They select and organize information to produce structured work, making appropriate use of dates and terms.

Level 6. Pupils use their factual knowledge and understanding of the history of Britain and other countries, drawn from the Key Stage 3 programme of study, to describe past societies and periods and to make links between features within and across periods. They examine, and are beginning to analyse the reasons for, and results of, events and changes. Pupils describe, and are beginning to explain, different historical interpretations of events, people and changes. Using their knowledge and understanding, they identify and evaluate sources of information, which they use critically to reach and support conclusions. They select, organize and deploy relevant information to produce structured work, making appropriate use of dates and terms.

Level 7. Pupils make links between their outline and detailed factual knowledge and understanding of the history of Britain and other countries drawn from the Key Stage 3 programme of study. They use this to analyse relationships between features of a particular period or society, and to analyse reasons for, and results of, events and changes. They explain how and why different historical interpretations have been produced. Pupils are beginning to show independence in following lines of enquiry, using their knowledge and understanding to identify, evaluate and use sources of information critically. They are beginning to reach substantiated conclusions independently. They select, organize and deploy relevant information to produce well-structured narratives, descriptions and explanations, making appropriate use of dates and terms.

Level 8. Pupils use their outline and detailed factual knowledge and understanding of the history of Britain and other countries, drawn from the Key Stage 3 programme of study, to analyse the relationships between events, people and changes, and between the features of past societies. Their explanations and analyses of, reasons for and results of events and changes are set in their wider historical context. They analyse and explain different historical interpretations and are beginning to evaluate them. Drawing on their historical knowledge and understanding, they use sources of information critically, carry out enquiries about historical topics and reach substantiated conclusions independently. They select, organize and deploy relevant information to produce consistently well-structured narratives, descriptions and explanations, making appropriate use of dates and terms.

Exceptional Performance. Pupils use their extensive and detailed factual knowledge and understanding of the history of Britain and other countries drawn from the Key Stage 3 programme of study, to analyse relationships between a wide range of events, people, ideas and changes, and between the features of past societies. Their explanations and analyses of, reasons for, and results of, events and changes are well substantiated and set in their wider historical context. They analyse links between events and developments that took place in different countries and in different periods. They make balanced judgements about the value of differing interpretations of historical events and developments in relation to their historical context. Drawing on their historical knowledge and understanding, they use sources of information critically, carry out enquiries about historical topics and reach and sustain substantiated and balanced conclusions independently. They select, organize and deploy a wide range of relevant information to produce consistently well-structured narratives, descriptions and explanations, making appropriate use of dates and terms.

Learning across the National Curriculum. The following is the introduction to the History part of the *National Curriculum for England* (QCA, 1999; www.nc.uk.net).

There are four sections in this introduction:
- Promoting pupils' spiritual, moral, social and cultural development through history.
- Promoting citizenship through history. History can play a significant part in promoting citizenship through, e.g. developing pupils' knowledge and understanding about political aspects of history including central and local government, the key characteristics of parliamentary and other forms of government, the development of the franchise, the role of national and international

organizations, and examples of different forms of action to effect change; providing opportunities for pupils to discuss the nature and diversity of societies in Britain and the wider world; developing pupils enquiry and communication skills; and, in particular, the ability to evaluate critically evidence and analyse interpretations.

- Promoting key skills through history – communication, application of number, IT, working with others, improving own learning and performance and problem-solving.
- Promoting other aspects of the curriculum – thinking skills; financial capability; education for sustainable development.

Lifelong Learning and the National Qualifications Framework. A broader vision of a national framework of qualifications for young people from age 14, and for adults, was outlined in the Green Papers on lifelong learning: 'The Learning Age', in England and Northern Ireland, and 'Learning is for Everyone', in Wales.

QCA, ACCAC and CCEA are responsible for developing a coherent national framework of academic and vocational qualifications. The framework is designed to: promote lifelong learning through clear routes of progression, supporting the achievement of national targets; promote access, motivation and attainment in education and training; avoid unnecessary duplication and overlap between qualifications, while ensuring sufficient breadth of provision to meet the full range of needs; and promote confidence in the relevance and integrity of national awards.

In addition, ministers have asked the regulatory authorities to explore the implications and the feasibility of moving towards a unitized or credit-based system as a way of increasing opportunities for adults and other part-time learners to study. A consultation has been undertaken by QCA and similar exercises are (at time of writing) underway in Wales and Northern Ireland.

In spring 1999, the regulatory authorities published the criteria forming the basis of accreditation of external qualifications in England, Wales and Northern Ireland. These will ensure that the quality, consistency and standards of national qualifications can be guaranteed across awarding bodies and over time. To be admitted to the national qualifications framework, qualifications must make an appropriate and distinctive contribution to the framework and meet the needs of users. It is intended that the national framework will be in place by September 2001.

Entry Level. The introduction of entry level, the initial level in the new national framework of qualifications, was a key recommendation arising from Lord Dearing's review in 1996. Entry level awards are for learners who are not yet ready for GCSE, foundation GNVQ or NVQ level 1. They are nationally recognized qualifications, accredited by QCA and its partner bodies in Wales and Northern

Ireland. There are three levels of achievement, which are broadly in line with National Curriculum levels 1–3.

Cooper, P. and McIntyre, D. (1996) *Effective Teaching and Learning*. Buckingham: Open University Press. A piece of research which seeks to understand the craft knowledge of teachers and pupils in the context of the National Curriculum in English and History at Key Stage 3.

DfEE (1995) *History in the National Curriculum (England)*. HMSO, Dd 298, 344, C1620, 1/95. London: DfEE.

Goalen, P. (1998) 'The history curriculum and national identity'. *Curriculum*, **19**(1), 23–32.

Honeybone, M. (1990) 'The nature of history and the National Curriculum'. *TH*, **60**, July, 9–11.

Lee, P., Dickinson, A., Ashby, R. (1996) 'Project Chata: concerts of history and teaching approaches at Key Stages 2 and 3'. *TH*, **82**, January, 6–11.

NCC (1992) *History and Economic and Industrial Understanding at Key Stages 3 and 4*. York: National Curriculum Council.

Phillips, R. (1998) *History Teaching, Nationhood and the State*. London: Cassell. This book explores the politics of the 'great history debate' and explains why history became so controversial.

SCAA (1997) *Expectations in History at Key Stages 1 and 2*. London: School Curriculum Assessment Authority.

Wragg, E. (1996) *Parent's Guides to the National Curriculum*. London: Addison Wesley Longman.

National Foundation for Educational Research. The NFER exists for the improvement of education and training. It has not published any specific research on the teaching and learning of history but it does contain a valuable, and comprehensive, Register of Educational Research as well as a helpful library and information service.

The Mere, Upton Park, Slough, Berkshire SL1 2DQ. Tel: 01753 574123; fax: 01753 691632; e-mail: enquiries@nfer.ac.uk; website: http://www.nfer.ac.uk

nationalization. The policy of taking major industries into state control. It was once a central part of the British Labour Party's constitution, under Clause Four, which committed the Party to the common ownership of industry; but this has now (since 1995) been dropped. The root of nationalization is the Marxist materialistic conception which suggests that the development of human societies is determined by the methods of production people use to meet their needs. It assumes that if these are controlled by the state they will be improved.

See separate entries under **Labour Party** *and* **Marx**.

National Trust. The leading conservation body in Britain, founded by Octavia Hill in 1895, 'to preserve places of historic interest and natural beauty'. It is independent of government and relies on voluntary contributions. There are more than 2 million subscribing members. It is national in the sense that it works on behalf of the nation. It owns more that 232,000 hectares, has protective rights over 31,500 hectares, 160 gardens, many of international importance, 60 villages and hamlets, farms and woodland, wind and water mills, prehistoric and Roman antiquities, nature reserves, a cotton mill and 230 houses open to the public, including 90 large country houses and castles, and 47 buildings associated with famous people. Perhaps the greatest treasures are the open countryside in Snowdonia, the Lake District, the Peak District, Clumber and Ashridge. Courses are held for young volunteers who work on the buildings and gardens, 'and in so doing imbibe, absorb and assimilate a sense of history, time, place, period and style' (Howard Newton (ed.) *The National Trust: The Next Hundred Years*, London, National Trust, 1995).

nation state.   Nationhood is not a legal concept but a subjective one. The idea of the nation state gradually emerged out of the American and French Revolutions. Only then did people begin to realize that the increased demands being made upon people would require a higher degree of political organization. The nation became recognized as the foundation of the legitimacy of the state; a marriage that had three consequences: first, the nation state was the recipe for success; secondly, many nation states became part of multinational empires and then tried to establish independent nation states of their own; and thirdly, all inhabitants of nation states became full members of them.

The break-up of the Romanov, Hohenzollern and Habsburg Empires, after the 1914–18 war, encouraged the principle of self-determination and hence the right for a nation state to run its own political affairs.

After the 1939–45 war, the boundaries in Europe looked very different from the way they do now. Germany was partitioned and eastern Europe was dominated by the USSR. The movement towards increased federalism has not abolished the nation state. Within several areas there has been a growing movement towards increased diversity – in Brittany, Basque Spain, Scotland and French-speaking Canada.

A student debate on a motion that 'Nationalism is the unacceptable expression of patriotism' is a helpful way of appreciating both views. Advocates of nationalism will suggest that it unites a country, enables decisions to be made and has a clear meaning. Advocates of patriotism will argue that it is the expression of feelings of loyalty and devotion to a country and is 'in tune' with the feelings of the people.

Kurt Hahn (1886–1974), the educational innovator and philosopher, regarded nationalism as the unacceptable face of patriotism. Albert Einstein (1879–1955) would have agreed; he said, 'Nationalism is an infantile sickness. It is the measles of the human race' (Helen Dukas and Banesh Hoffman, *Albert Einstein: The Human Side*, 1979).

Axtmann, R. (1996) *Liberal Democracy into the Twenty First Century: Globalisation, Integration, and the Nation-State*. Manchester: Manchester University Press.
Lord Beloff (1993) 'The nation-state'. *MHR*, **4**(3), February, 9–10.
Milward, A. S. (1992) *The European Rescue of the Nation-State*. London: Routledge.

newspapers. Newspapers offer us a contemporary account of events that happened. Nowadays many newspapers have facilities for supplying back issues. Newspapers have some specific uses: they highlight events and emphasize the flavour of an occasion such as D-Day, 6 June 1944. They can represent a period in themselves and become 'icons', e.g. the early layouts of *The Times*. If it is possible to share accounts between different newspapers some useful contrasts can be drawn, as in the reporting of general election results. Sometimes, newspaper accounts are important enough to warrant careful textual analysis, as with the abdication of Edward VIII, Princess Diana's funeral or the invasion of Kosovo. Perhaps the most significant point about newspapers is that they can provide a human dimension to what would otherwise be a purely factual account. As with photographs, newspaper accounts can stress the bravery and the poignancy of a particular event and create a sense of stark reality.

Murphy, M. J. (1991) *Newspapers and Local History*. Chichester: Phillimore.
Wilkinson, G. R. (1991) 'Sources: newspapers'. *MHR*, **3**(2), 14–15.

Newton. Isaac Newton (1642–1727) demonstrated that the key to understanding lay in rational thought and experimentation. In a real sense the scientific age began with him.

Principia Mathematica gave us his method of 'fluxious' or calculus, his universal law of gravitation and his three laws of motion:

Law 1: Every body continues in its state of rest, or of uniform motion in a right line, unless it is compelled to change that state by forces impressed upon it.

Law 2: The change of motion is proportional to the motive force impressed; and is made in the direction of the right line in which that force is impressed.

Law 3: To every action there is always opposed and equal reaction: or, the mutual actions of two bodies upon each other are always equal, and directed to contrary parts.

Newton himself said: 'At the first perusal of my book it is enough if you understand the Propositions with some of the Demonstration (proofs) which are easier than the rest. For when you understand the easier, they will afterwards give you light into the harder.' The *Principia* was a landmark in the history of science and on thinking generally, especially in the eighteenth century.

Jardine, L. (1999) *Ingenious Pursuits: Building the Scientific Revolution*. Boston, MA: Little, Brown.
Newton, I. (1999) (trans. B. Cohen and A. Whitman) *Principia Mathematica 1687*. Berkeley, CA: University of California Press.

North Atlantic Treaty Organisation. NATO was created on 4 April 1949, in Washington DC. The original signatories were the USA, the UK, Canada, Belgium, Luxemburg, The Netherlands, France, Italy, Norway, Denmark, Iceland and Portugal. Greece and Turkey joined in 1952, West Germany in 1955, Spain in 1982, Hungary in 1998 and the Czechoslovak Republic in 1999.

It was formed in response to fears about possible and, some felt, likely Russian expansion into western Europe and a serious intensification of the existing Cold War. The North Atlantic Treaty stated that an attack on one was an attack on all. Significantly, it coupled the USA with western Europe. It remained a defensive alliance until NATO bombed Serbia in May 1999 in order to deter President Milosovic from the ethnic removal of Moslems from Kosovo; this was the first campaign in which NATO had acted offensively, with eleven weeks of serial bombing.

The rival organization in eastern Europe was the Warsaw Pact, which was eventually dissolved, and the Malta Summit of NATO leaders meeting in June 1989 declared the Cold War at an end.

The future of NATO was discussed by Kofi Annan, the Secretary-General of the United Nations, in the 50th anniversary celebration booklet:

> NATO has made a vital contribution to regional stability in Europe, most recently in Bosnia and Herzegovina, where I have the honour to transfer responsibility from UNPROFOR (the United Nations Protection Force) to the NATO-led Implementation Force under the Dayton Agreement of December 1995 ... And, should the Security Council ever again have to authorise enforcement action in Europe or North America, under Chapter VII of the Charter, I know that the skills and resources of NATO will prove invaluable.

Students may not all be aware of NATO, the Warsaw Pact, the Iron Curtain or Kosovo, and it is probably enough, and important in the present climate, to provide a historical context comparable to the one outlined above. Part of the problem in explaining NATO is not always about total ignorance but about misunderstanding and misinterpretation.

Lello, J. (1993) 'NATO, hindsight' (GCSE *Modern History Review*), **3**(3), April. 18–21.

NATO (1989) *North Atlantic Treaty Organisation: Facts and Figures*. Brussels. 50th Anniversary Commemorative Edition.

O

Office for Standards in Education. OFSTED is a government department but is independent of the Department for Education and Employment. It is a product of the Education (Schools) Act 1992, which restructured Her Majesty's Inspectorate. The position of Senior Chief Inspector was replaced by Her Majesty's Chief Inspector of Schools (OHCMCI). The role of OFSTED is to improve standards of achievement and quality in education through inspection, reporting and advice. Schools are inspected regularly within a national framework and a report is published after each inspection. Inspections are carried out by teams of independent inspectors contracting for work under a system of competitive tendering.

OFSTED, Alexandra House, 33 Kingsway, London WC2B 6SE. Tel: 0207 421 6800; website: www.ofsted.gov.uk

Lomas, T. (1994) 'A Guide to preparing the history curriculum in primary schools for an OFSTED inspection'. Occasional Paper 8. London: HA.
OFSTED (1992–3) *Implementation of the Curriculum Requirements of the Education Reform Act.* London: HMSO.
OFSTED (1993–4) *Review of Inspection Findings.* London: HMSO. *Teaching History,* **80**, June 1995.

oral tradition. Largely centred on working-class testimony from the nineteenth and twentieth centuries. Some of it is politically partisan or unbalanced, but it nevertheless provides an additional source of information about the past which, when juxtaposed with other material, can illuminate and enhance existing records. Originally, oral history was part of the History Workshop movement led by Raphael Samuel.

George Ewart Evans, one of the pioneers of writing oral history in Britain and Ireland, wrote:

> The historian, at the end of the twentieth century, needs to widen his catchment area to include the material revealed by anthropologists all

over the world, in order to make a closer bond between the disciplines. No longer does the historian study documents only, while the anthropologist concentrates on people. Oral history is quickly developing into a fruitful amalgam of both approaches. (G. E. Evans (1987) *Spoken History*. London: Faber and Faber)

Much of the oral history that Evans and others describes comes from recording eye-witness accounts on audio tape. These have come from people of all ages, but are predominantly old people's accounts of their younger years. These recordings are not very difficult to make, and it is of special significance that they contain no interruptions, leading questions, or subtle annotation, once the person is speaking. Sometimes, when the flow is unbroken, the speaker will move into areas which would not have been expected. It is therefore important for the person with the microphone to be patient, not to prompt, and to realize that the material being collected is the object of the exercise. There are still vast untapped sources of historical material and it is material that young people can often help to uncover, especially if they come from large families with older relations still living or if they are prepared to seek out suitable people in the area where they live, or in the church they attend. If, however, young people are to act as interviewers it is very important that they receive some advice on impartial interviewing before they start.

The Oral History Society has 1000 members worldwide who receive the journal *Oral History* twice yearly, can meet other oral-history enthusiasts at conferences and have access to a network of representative and affiliated groups all over Britain.

Oral History Society, c/o Department of Sociology, University of Essex, Wivenhoe Park, Colchester CO4 3SQ. Website: www.essex.ac.uk/sociology/oralhis.htm

National Sound Archive Oral History, British Library, 96 Euston Road, London NW1 2DB. Services offered include a specialist curator, training days in interview techniques and films and seminars. They have a catalogue of oral history holdings, issue several publications and have close contact with the Oral History Society's regional network. Tel: 0207 412 7440; fax: 0207 412 7441; e-mail: NSA-oral@bl.uk; website: www.uk/collections/sound-archive/oral.html

Cramer, I. (1993) 'Oral history: working with children'. *TH*, **71**, April, 17–19.
Evans, G. E. (1993) *The Crooked Scythe: An Anthology of Oral History*. London: Faber.
Redfern, A. (1995) *Talking in Class: Oral History and the National Curriculum*. Colchester: Oral History Society.
Weiler, K. and Middleton, S. (1999) *Telling Women's Lives*. Oxford: OUP.

P

parliamentary democracy. Bagehot, writing in 1867, believed there was a choice between a presidential and a parliamentary form of government. The development of the particular British form of democracy developed throughout the nineteenth century with the gradual widening of the franchise and the gradual decline of the powers of the monarch. It went hand-in-hand with growing industrialization, but the changes were modest at first; the 1832 Act only increased the electorate from 500,000 to 813,000. Nevertheless, it encouraged the growth of political parties, and the Conservative and Liberal parties changed into mass-membership parties which gave a larger number of people a voice and eventually included women (in 1928) over the age of 21. In 1969 voting was extended to all 18–21-year-olds. However, all these changes were strongly contested and were often seen as threats to the constitution and to property. The essential characteristic of parliamentary democracy is that there is party government which needs the support of a majority to operate. Bagehot would have preferred 'an assembly of detached and independent men', and so the present party-political system might have seemed less than ideal to him.

The best teaching example is to follow, with care and precise analysis, the working of a local or national election in the UK. This will not make the students political or apolitical, but it will reveal the essential workings of the complicated British political system. A visit to a local Council, or the House of Commons, is a good follow-up exercise.

Bagehot, W. (1867) *1826–77: The English Constitution.*
Morris, A. J. (1967) *Parliamentary Democracy in the Nineteenth Century.* Oxford: Pergamon.
Norton P. (ed.) (1990) *Legislatures.* Oxford: OUP.
Norton, P. (1991) 'Parliamentary democracy'. *MHR,* **2**(3), 22–3.

patch. This approach, introduced by Marjorie Reeves, is where a topic is chosen, not necessarily a period. For example, a project on the wheel could start with its invention, continue with its use on chariots, water mills, coaches, buses, cars, aeroplanes and so on. Any inclusion which involved the wheel in some way, say the mechanism of a clock, would be acceptable. The patch method was once more popular than it is currently, although many primary schools still use the patch in teaching history or any other comparable body of knowledge. It does enable the natural and easy continuation of subjects because it overrides subject boundaries. It appeals to the acquisitive instinct of many children who like to collect. It is useful in **mixed-ability teaching** because it caters for the different speeds at which children work. It is a method which can be used with minimal resources and although this is not ideal when a lot of material is available, it is nevertheless possible to engage pupils' interest with quite modest resource provision. Scholarly work is possible with the patch because the student who becomes very involved in a piece of history can pursue the interest to quite an advanced level.

There are at least four reasons why it is not always a valuable method: it can ignore chronology and can therefore confuse; it can be used too often and therefore become tiresome; it is time-consuming to guide and correct; it requires intensive teacher involvement and can thus become a non-stop exercise. Nevertheless, it should not be totally discarded.

Fairley, J. A. (1970) *Patch History and Creativity*. London: Longman.
Palmer, J. and Pettit, D. (1993) *Topic Work in the Early Years*. London: Routledge.
Reeves, M. (1980) *Why History?* Harlow: Longman.

philosophy of history. This falls into three categories: there are the substantive or speculative philosophers who consider history in the sense of the past. These include Kant, who considered that nature should be ordered in such a way as to be intelligible and purposive; **Hegel**, the objective idealist; **Marx**; and Arnold Toynbee, who favoured a scientific approach to human affairs and civilization in his *magnum opus*, *A Study of History*, written between 1934 and 1954.

Another group consists of analytical or critical philosophers who look at history as a study of the past and interest themselves with evidence or explanation. These include Benedetto Croce (1866–1952), who regarded historical thought as the re-creation of past experience. He influenced greatly Robin George Collingwood (1889–1943), who believed the historian's task was to 'rethink' or 'inwardly re-enact' the deliberation of past agents which renders their behaviour intelligible. Reconstructing the thoughts that lay behind, or were embodied in, historical actions was at the heart of Collingwood's *Idea of History*.

The last category consists of those who narrate the antecedents of what is to be explained. This narrative approach was chosen by Herbert Butterfield (1900–79) in his books *A Whig Interpretation of History* and *History of Science*. In the same position was Michael Oakeshott (1901–92), whose book *Rationalisation in Politics* (1962) held that reality was shown to us in a number of human practices of which history was one; he did not, however, believe that this reality could be reduced to a formula or analysed in terms of extrinsic goals.

The best way to consider the philosophy of history, or any philosophy, is to philosophize, and this is exceedingly difficult unless the essential skills have been acquired. A substitute is to study passages of the original texts of the philosophers concerned, but these will not be of much value unless they are accompanied by informed discussion. There is genuine scope if students can meet in an informal situation, at home or in a club. Teacher and taught should come having read beforehand, and bring the relevant texts and notes they have made before the general discussion; an introductory paper, however short, is a useful primer to the discussion pump. A traditional, but valuable, conclusion to such an exercise is to make the discussion the basis for a weekly essay, though it might be less inhibiting for students if this was announced at the end.

'Philosophy consists very largely of one philosopher arguing that all others are jackasses. He usually proves it, and I should add that he usually proves that he is one himself' (H. L. Mencken (1880–1956) *Minority Report*, 1956).

Beloff, M. (1992) *An Historian in the Twentieth Century.* New Haven, CT: Yale University Press.
Elton, G.R. (1967) *The Practice of History.* London: Sydney University Press.
Jenkins, K. (1995) *What is History?* London: Routledge.
Walsh, W. H. (1967) *An Introduction to the Philosophy of History.* London: Hutchinson.

photography. 'Photography is truth', wrote Jean-Luc Godard, the French director, but the comment would have been better put as a question. The camera can lie, distort or represent one untypical second, but is always interesting and fascinating. Old photographs can sometimes be more revealing than words; the poignancy of the wedding photo of the Duke of Windsor at least equals, if not eclipses, his abdication speech. Many students are the inheritors of a treasury of family photographs – of weddings, military service or childhood. Fortunately, it is possible to have these old prints restored to something like their previous clarity, thus making them easy to inspect and share.

Photographs of a family are usually valuable to that family, but photographs of a street at different times can often show clearly the development of a community. In these ways photographs can help to show the growth and history of a society, and if ground photos can be viewed in conjunction with **aerial photographs** the coverage will be so much richer.

An interesting comparison can be made, for example, between the photos of the Crimean War, during which photos were first used to record war, and the later photos of the Vietnam or Korean wars. The Crimean record does not show the full horrors of war, as do more modern examples.

See separate entry on **aerial photography**.

Grosvenor, I., Lawn, M. and Rousmaniere, K. (1999) *Silences and Images*. New York: Lang.
Harrison, B. (1989) 'Visual history?' *MHR*, **1**(2), November, 31–3.
Lister, M. (ed.) (1995) *The Photographic Image in Digital Culture*. London: Routledge.

political parties.   The expression of particular interest, power and opinion in a country. Most democracies contain several parties, and the one with the most popular support, according to the peculiarities of the **voting system** preferred, forms the government.

In Britain there are three main parties – Conservative, Labour and Liberal Democrat – but, in addition, the three separate, partially self-governing countries of the United Kingdom contain other regional parties. Scotland has a significant representation of the Scottish Nationalist Party in their Parliament, and Wales of the Welsh Nationalist Party, Plaid Cymru. In Ulster, the largest party is the Ulster Unionist Party, but the Democratic Unionist Party is also represented. Sinn Fein, the party advocating a united Ireland, is often supported by the Social Democratic Labour Party, although both are quite separate.

In other countries there are usually several parties involved in an election. The United States has the Republican and Democratic parties, who were once amusingly described by Alistair Cooke as being like: 'Two bottles, different labels, both empty.'

China has one party, like other communist countries, which is all-embracing and avoids the necessity for any political turbulence which might disturb their more cherished economic democracy. Mexico now has several parties, but until recently there was really only one party called PRI, which was an umbrella party covering as many contrasting shades of political opinion as you would expect to find in several parties elsewhere.

British political parties are usually pleased to send details of their current policies and programmes and are prepared to suggest suitable speakers for a political forum or discussion. At election times a school or college is often anxious to stage a mock general election of its own, with internal candidates, posters and hustings, and culminating in a voting system. Sometimes the voting can be arranged using a 'first-past-the-post' method, or with proportional representation, so that contrasted methods can be observed in practice. But any mock election can be dangerous; from a purely political viewpoint, the arguments portrayed are often pale imitations of the policy which is being projected nationally.

Lijphart, A. (1994) *Electoral Systems and Party Systems*. Oxford: OUP.

political philosophy.   The political philosophy of a country seeks to keep in balance theoretical concepts like autonomy, self-determination, justice, democracy, rights, political obligation and so on: the existence of, or the proportions of, these concepts in the organization of a country is what distinguishes one country from another.

Some great philosophers have grappled with the political nature of society:

Philosopher	Major work(s)
Plato BC 427–347	*Republic* c.380–70
Aristotle BC 384–22	*Politics* c.350–23
St Augustine AD 354–430	*City of God*
St Thomas Aquinas 1224/5–74	*Summa Theologiae*
Thomas Hobbes 1588–1679	*Leviathan* (1651)
John Locke 1632–1704	*First Treatise on Government; Second Treatise* (1690)
Jean-Jacques Rousseau 1712–78	*Social Contract* (1762)
John Stuart Mill 1806–73	'On Liberty' (1859) *Considerations*
Georg Hegêl 1770–1831	*Lectures on the Philosophy of World History*
Karl Marx 1818–83	*Das Kapital* (1867); *Communist Manifesto* (1868)
Friedrich Engels 1820–95	*Conditions: the Working Years in England* (1845)
Isaiah Berlin 1909–99	*Four Essays on Liberty* (1969)

A sixth-form exercise to tackle this complicated subject is for individual students to prepare a short biographical introduction to a particular philosopher. The teacher explains the philosophy of the particular individual. To conclude each dual exposition, a handout is issued to the class.

Honderich, E. (1995) *The Oxford Companion to Philosophy*. Oxford: OUP.

poor law.   The Poor Laws were designed to provide relief for the poor. An Act, in 1536, gave relief for those who could not work but compelled 'sturdy beggars' to work. The money came from voluntary subscriptions and was administered by the parish. In 1552 parish registers were introduced and this legislation was refined in 1597 and 1601, when justices of the peace were given overall responsibility, including the responsibility for raising funds. The 1662 Act permitted Overseers of the Poor to send vagrants back to their native parishes. Grinding poverty still prevailed and in most areas it got worse. After 1795, the Speenhamland system was adopted; it supplemented labourers' wages according to wheat prices and the size of their families, and had the effect of depressing wage levels, reducing incentives to save and delaying marriages. The 1834 Poor Law Amendment Act created 600 unions of parishes, managed by Boards of Guardians who were elected by ratepayers. Outdoor relief ceased and paupers were forced into the workhouse where conditions were intentionally harsh in order to deter malingerers. The workhouse became a stigma. Slowly, in the twentieth century, the system was dismantled and old-age pensions and a comprehensive package of social security replaced the Poor Laws. In spite of all the massive changes wrought by the Welfare State, the stigma of having to accept help from the workhouse never fully died and was always keenly felt.

The main problem with teaching the history of the poor law is having to portray the pain and indignity; it is hard to convey hunger, suffering and cruelty. Yet these harsh sentiments are a part of the history of the poor law and the context in which it operated. Sometimes it is possible to obtain a feel for what it must have been like by visiting an old workhouse. Such an experience is becoming rare, and even where former workhouses remain they have been transformed out of all recognition. An easier route is to try to obtain a copy of the rules, programme or diet of a nineteenth-century workhouse from a record office, from which the flavour can be more fully appreciated.

Boyer, G. R. (1990) *An Economic History of the English Poor Law.* Cambridge: CUP.
Dickens, C. (1837) *Oliver Twist.*

presidents of the United States of America. These are a varied bunch, and some have been outstanding. All have taken the Oath of Office: 'I do solemnly swear (or affirm) that I will faithfully execute the Office of President of the United States, and will to the best of my ability, preserve, protect and defend the Constitution of the United States.'

The qualifications for the Office of President are in the Constitution, Article II, Section 1, Paragraph 5:

> No person except a natural born Citizen, or a Citizen of the United States, at the time of the Adoption of this Constitution, shall be eligible for the office who shall not have attained to the Age of thirty five years, and have been fourteen years a resident within the United States.

Some of the more famous of the 42 are as follows (major incidents during their presidential tenure are listed):

Washington (1732–99) came from a well-established Virginian planter family, had reached the rank of Colonel in the army and was elected Commander-in-Chief at the Second Continental Congress. He drove the British out of Boston in 1776, and later, after several military victories and with the support of the French in 1780, succeeded in the victory at Yorktown which ended the war. He had thus successfully held his army together and soon supported the Constitution. Elected to the presidency unanimously and then re-elected a second time. He called for neutrality in foreign affairs. Rightly described as the father of his nation he had a clear sense of direction and purpose during the confused and confusing early days of the USA.

Thomas Jefferson (1743–1826) drafted the Declaration of Independence while he was Governor of the State of Virginia during the War of Independence. He was instrumental in arranging the Louisiana Purchase from France in 1803. He was a believer in the virtues of an agrarian republic and a weak central government.

Abraham Lincoln (1809–65) was born in Kentucky and moved with his parents to Illinois. He was elected to Congress in 1846 and eventually joined the Republican Party. He became the spokesman for the federal union and for an anti-slavery programme. He was fatally wounded by John Wilkes Booth.

Woodrow Wilson (1856–1924) had been Governor of New Jersey. He eventually supported the USA entering the 1914–18 war. At the end of the war he proposed the Fourteen Points as a basis for peace. He strongly supported the League of Nations.

Franklin Delano Roosevelt (1882–1945) had been Governor of New York State. One of the main features of his presidency was the New Deal programme which was an imaginative package of social and agrarian reforms. He had always fought isolationism in his own country, but it was the bombing of the American fleet in Pearl Harbor by the Japanese in 1941 that persuaded the Americans to enter the Second World War.

Dwight Eisenhower (1890–1969) was a former general and represented what he called 'new modern Republicanism'. He reduced taxes, balanced budgets, decreased federal control and, in foreign affairs, sought reconciliation with China and the Soviet Union.

John Fitzgerald Kennedy (1917–63) was a Democratic senator for Massachusetts. He was very popular, and many people, inside and outside the USA, saw him as the hope for the future of the western world. He resisted Kruschev during the Cuban Missile Crisis in 1962 and negotiated a test-ban treaty in 1963. However, it was his decision to send American troops to Vietnam that subsequently proved to be a major problem for his successor Lyndon Johnson. Kennedy was assassinated in 1963.

primary school history.   The specific teaching of history in primary schools is more related to entries in this book like **toys**. By the same token, some of the topics would be inapplicable to younger students. However, the relevance to the teacher of other concepts like Piaget's stages of learning, outlined in this book, are important, whether the whole of the Piaget's psychology is embraced or not. The baseline for many practical approaches and development in primary schools is the HMI Report, *Aspects of Primary Education: The Teaching and Learning of History and Geography* (DES/HMSO).

Blyth, J. (1989) *History in Primary Schools*. Buckingham: OU Press.
Cooper, H. (1992) *The Teaching of History* (Studies in Primary Education). London: Fulton.
Davies, J. (1986) 'Artifacts in the primary school'. *TH*, **45**, June, 6–8.
DES (1990) *History for Ages 5–16: Proposals of the Secretary of State for Education and Science*. London: HMSO.
Huggins, M. and Knight, P. (1997) 'Curriculum continuity and transfer from primary to secondary school: the case for history'. *Educational Studies*, **23**(3), November, 333–48.
NCC (1991) *History Non-Statutory Guidance*. London: National Curriculum Council.
Pond, M. and Childs, A. (1995) 'Do children learn from "Living History" projects?' *CJ*, **6**(1), Spring, 47–62.

projects.   Encourage children to undertake research assignments into historical topics. Children are able to work at their own speed, develop their own interests and exercise considerable personal choice. As a result, well-organized projects can arouse enthusiasm in pupils and the teacher has a consultative, guiding and stimulating role rather than a purely didactic one.

The Dalton Plan is an extreme form of this technique and involves cutting through subject specializations and, therefore, through the timetable.

See separate entries on **group work**, **mixed-ability teaching** *and the* **patch**.

Central Advisory Council for Education (England) (1967) *Children and their Primary Schools* (the Plowden Report). London: HMSO.
Ferguson, S. (1967) *Projects in History*. London: Batsford.
Waters, D. (1982) *Primary School Projects*. London: Heinemann.

propaganda.   Consists of exaggerated or false information circulated to influence people's opinions and attitudes; this often includes deliberate distortion or over-emphasis. It is intentional, and powerful, as in Goebbels's work in Nazi Germany and Mussolini's in Italy.

In democratic countries comparable propaganda also exists, as in Franklin Roosevelt's New Deal policy in the USA. Whatever the specific example, the one common feature is the control, or attempted control, of the media.

Beevor, A. (1998) *Stalingrad: The CIA and the Cultural Cold War.* Harmondsworth: Viking Penguin.

Saunders, F. S. (1999) *Who Paid the Piper?* London: Granta.

website: powers of persuasion http://www.nava.gov/exhall/powers/powershtml

Q

Qualifications and Curriculum Authority. Created in 1997 as a result of the amalgamation of the School Curriculum and Assessment Authority (SCAA) with the National Council for Vocational Qualifications (NCVQ). It is to oversee the curriculum, assessment and qualifications offered in schools, colleges and the workplace and is the regulatory authority for all awarding bodies.

R

radio. 'Steam' radio is not as commonly used in schools and colleges as it was some 20 years ago. Then, it was usual for some schools, primary and secondary, to construct the timetable around the timing of radio programmes. This still happens to some extent because the programmes are good and because the BBC Schools Broadcasting Service circulates details of what will be available in order to assist teachers in planning lessons.

A main element in radio usage is Open University courses, which are often broadcast at inconvenient times but are easily taped and provide first-rate written materials from established academics who are well-practised in using the medium.

See also **sound libraries.**

Reformation and Counter-Reformation. A convenient starting point for this movement for the reform of the doctrines and practices of the Roman Catholic Church is 1517, when Martin **Luther** nailed his protest against the corruption and power of the Roman Catholic Church to the door of the church at Wittenberg. There had been earlier criticism of the structure of the Church beforehand, by Wyclif, but Luther's had a much greater and more permanent effect.

Luther himself attacked the corruption of the papacy and sought to return to the simplicity of the early Church. He attacked transubstantiation, celibacy and papal supremacy and advocated a reform of the religious orders.

Zwingli led the Reformation in Zurich and his Protestant leadership in Switzerland passed to **Calvin**.

The Roman Catholic Church's answer to the Protestant Reformation had three main aspects: it led to a reformation of the papacy by Pius V (1566–72) with the intention of creating a more spiritual outlook; it encouraged the foundation of new religious orders like the Oratorians and the Society of Jesus (1540) and led to the reform of the Capuchins and the Franciscans; and it led directly to the summoning of the Council of Trent (1545–63), which defined and clarified Catholic doctrine on most points of dispute with Protestants.

This Counter-Reformation in the mid-sixteenth to mid-seventeenth centuries became political through links with Philip II of Spain who sought to re-establish Roman Catholicism by force. It was called the Thirty Years War and was brought to an end by the Treaty of Westphalia in 1648, which concluded the Counter-Reformation.

Clark, F. (1972) *The Reformation*. Bletchley: Open University.
Kidd, B. J. (1933) *Counter Reformation*. London: SPCK.
website: The Protestant Reformation – http://history.hanover.edu/early/prot.html
website: The Catholic Reformation – http://history.hanover.edu/early/cath.html

Renaissance. The Renaissance emerged slowly in the fourteenth century as an intellectual and artistic reawakening. It continued throughout the fifteenth century and into the sixteenth century. It took the classical civilizations of Greece and Rome as its root. These aspects had been neglected during the Middle Ages and needed to be revived. Man was thought to be limitless in the things he could achieve, and was exalted by Leo Battista Alberti, Leonardo da Vinci, the architect Brunelleschi, Pisano, the sculptor Donatello and many others. Other painters were faithful to nature while introducing perspective; they included Giotto, Masaccio, Michelangelo, Raphael and Titian.

The centres of the Renaissance in the fifteenth and sixteenth centuries were Florence, Venice, Rome, Mantua, Urbino and Ferraro. In all of these cities, rulers like the Medicis and the popes were essential patrons. Soon the ideals and spirit of the Renaissance spread to other parts of Europe, especially to the north, and to Germany through Albrecht Dürer. Literature in the vernacular blossomed; both in Italy, with writers like Dante, Petrarch and Boccacio; and outside, with Erasmus (Netherlands), Montaigne and Rabelais (France), Lope de Vega and Cervantes (Spain), and Spenser, Sydney, Shakespeare and Bacon (England). It was greatly helped by the invention of printing, which enabled more than a restricted number of scholars to read books.

At the same time, great voyages of discovery were taking place by Diaz de Novaes, Da Gama and Magellan. These led to advances in geography, cartography, astronomy and science. The voyages also led to colonization, imperialism and overseas governmental structures based on European models.

While these ideas were fermenting and exploding there was a

comparable spirit of change developing in the Church (*see separate entry on the* **Reformation**).

To bring the Renaissance alive it is well worth visiting Italy, preferably Florence, Venice or Rome. If this is not possible, then a visit to any major gallery, like the National Gallery, is essential. It would be sad, and would make the Renaissance hard to appreciate, if all the paintings studied were seen only as reproductions.

Huyghe, R. (1968) *Larousse Encyclopaedia of Renaissance.* London: Hamlyn.
Kraye, J. (1996) *The Cambridge Companion to Renaissance.* London and New York: CUP.

Royal Historical Society. Founded in 1868 and received the title 'Royal' in 1887. Its aim is to promote the study of history by publishing documentary material and bibliographical and reference works. These include the Transactions of Papers delivered at meetings and conferences, the Camden Series of unpublished texts, guides and handbooks for historians, an annual *Bibliography of British and Irish History* and a series of historical monographs. The Society also arranges a varied programme of lectures and conferences. The office and library are located in University College London, Gower Street, London WC1E 6BT. Tel. and fax: 0207 387 7532. The Society is governed by a Council and there is an Executive Secretary.

Royal Society. The Royal Society is the world's oldest scientific academy. Founded in 1660, its Fellowship has continued to make significant contributions to scientific progress through meetings, research, experiment and published reports in the journal *Philosophical Transactions*, and in the publication *Notes and Records*.

It has a library, dating from 1660, and an unrivalled collection of scientific books, journals and manuscripts. It has maintained detailed records, including proceedings of ordinary meetings and scientific correspondence. One of its treasures is Newton's *Principia Mathematica*.

'The history of science represents a very important element and perhaps even the core of scientific culture and should be integrated into every curriculum' (Claude Debru, Centre Européen d'Histoire de la Medicine, and quoted in the publicity leaflet for *Notes and Records*).

The Royal Society for the Promotion of Natural Knowledge, 6 Carlton House Terrace, London, SW1Y 5AG. Tel: 0207 839 5561; fax: 0207 976 1837.

S

Schools Council History Project. The SCHP catered for the 13–16 age range and then added the 9–13 group. The project, led by David Sylvester, was a pioneering venture in 1976. He believed history was a subject about people – their sayings, deeds and past sufferings. History involved detective work and the search for evidence, which took several forms, but could be separated into primary and secondary sources. History often involved asking questions about actions, motives and the consequences of deeds. This raised important issues about bias, different interpretations and insufficient evidence.

Shemilt, D. (1976) *History 13–16: Evaluation Study.* Glasgow: Holmes McDougall.
Sylvester, D. (1976) *A New Look at History 13–16* (the Schools Council History Project). Glasgow: Holmes McDougall.
Williams, N. (1986) *Schools Council History Project 13–16* (with bibliography). *TH*, **46**, October, 8–12.

scramble for Africa. The phrase used in the late nineteenth century to describe the acquisition of African land by the European powers. The Berlin Conferences (1884–5) called by Bismarck, and including representatives of all the European nations, the USA and Turkey, were an important stage in the partition of Africa. Britain recognized the German claims to the Cameroons and, in return, won the support of Bismarck against French competition in Nigeria. Britain also retained Sierra Leone and an interest in Southern Africa. A Conference in Brussels, in 1890, settled the outlines of the new states and resulted in the drawing of those straight frontier lines in Africa that still exist, but which were made without consulting the inhabitants. Eventually, the whole of Africa was partitioned by the imperial powers, including the USA which obtained a foothold in Liberia. A convenient partial resolution to this 'scramble' came in 1902 with the conclusion of the Second Boer War, but the international competition it had aroused was a contributing factor leading to the outbreak of war in 1914.

A graphic way of looking at these events is to place a series of maps, covering 100 years, onto the OHP. The last map must be an up-to-date version. This cartographic sequence will illustrate clearly the 'carving up' of the continent.

Behind this graphic representation lies a sophisticated world of European diplomacy. For many reasons, to do with economic expansion and political power, the possession of colonies became the expression of international strength and importance. It was happening all over the world, but nowhere more transparently than in Africa.

There is a positive side to colonization which, to some extent, balances imperial aggrandisement: improved trade brought prosperity, work and associated rewards such as schools, medical services and an improved administrative infrastructure. Slowly, the beginnings of a different colonial lifestyle were laid, albeit with the removal or a sublimation of most of the native tribal structures. It is easy to criticize the territorial acquisitiveness of the European nations, but students should be encouraged to seek a balanced view.

Pakenham, T. (1991) *The Scramble for Africa*. London: Random House.

science.   The history of science needs an historian to put it into the correct perspective in the curriculum. It needs a scientist to explain, preferably with demonstrations in a laboratory, what it is about. Science history provides a context within which a student can observe, reason and check conclusions reached, and is not merely concerned with imparting facts, important though they may be.

The word 'science' means 'to know'. The scientific method consists of testing constantly the viability of theories until they can be permanently included. This search for new facts and principles is called pure science, and the application of them is called applied science. Both pure and applied science have many branches, and many overlap with each other. There is an underlying overall unity between these different subjects and, with all of them, the additional common factor is mathematics.

The history of science is developing at a very fast rate. A useful source is the Science Museum. STEM (Students' and Teachers' Educational Materials) was developed on the Internet to encourage teachers and students to make use of the Science Museum on-line, and to share ideas that include the history of science.

Contact Martin Bazley at the Science Museum (0207 938 8096); e-mail: m.bazley@hmsi.ac.uk; website: http://www.hmsi.ac.uk/education/stem

The other equally valuable mine of information is the Natural

History Museum (see **museums (London)**): http://www.nhm.ac.uk; or contact the Teachers' Centre (0207 938 8744).

The Association for Science Education, College Lane, Hatfield, Herts (AL log AA). Tel: 01707 267411; fax: 01707 266532. They publish *Education in Science* and the *Primary Science Review*, and both of these regularly publish articles on the history of science.

Gribbin, J. (ed.) (1998) *A Brief History of Science*. London: Weidenfeld.
Harding, S. (1991) *Whose Science? Whose Knowledge?* Buckingham: OUP.
Hobhouse, H. (1999) *Standing on the Shoulders of Giants*. Burton: Kings School.
Keller, E. F. and Longino, H. (ed.) (1996) *Feminism and Science*. Oxford: OUP.
Usborne Illustrated Dictionary of Science (1999). London: Usborne.

See separate entry on **medicine**.

slave trade and slavery. The slave trade started in the mid-fifteenth century when the Portuguese imported Moors from North Africa (hence Blackamoor). As the Portuguese and Spanish empires in the Caribbean and on the mainland grew, so additional labour was needed. It was the establishment of the great staple commodities – sugar and tobacco – which required extra labour, and negroes were cheaper than indentured whites. By 1681 there were 2000 Negro slaves and by 1754 there were over a quarter of a million. The trade in slaves was made possible by the Asiento clause of the Peace of Ubrecht, 1713, and with it came the triangular trade between North America, Britain (London, Liverpool, Bristol and Glasgow) and West Africa. It seems possible that between 1801 and 1850, 3.2 million slaves were carried. Brazil had the highest number of slaves (4 million) and the British had 2.4 million. During the eighteenth century the slave trade was dominated by Britain, followed by Portugal and France. By the time of the Civil War there were approximately 4 million slaves in the USA.

Eventually the Quakers and William Wilberforce led a movement for the abolition of the slave trade, and it was finally abolished in 1807.

The emancipation of the slaves did not follow in Britain until 1833. Slightly later, in the American Civil War, the victory of the north led to the formal end to slavery in the USA, although many of the undesirable associations continued for many years. The expansion of the European countries into Africa slowly led to the end of slavery in that continent.

Marteilhe, J. (1957) (ed. K. Fenwick), *Galley Slave*. London: Folio.
Tattersfield, N. (1998) *The Forgotten Trade*. London: Pimlico.
Thomas, H. (1997) *The Slave Trade*. London: Picador.
There are numerous Key Stage 3 books and packs in *Living History Factfile*. British Library.

Smith, Adam.   Adam Smith (1723–90), FRS, was the Lord Rector of Glasgow University. He was a Scottish Free Trade economist whose major work *The Wealth of Nations* (1777) systematized economic ideas and ideas about economic development.

For this reason he is considered the founder of classical economics. He focused on the creation of wealth and noted the importance of manufacturing industry as well as agriculture. He argued that to increase wealth, division of labour and a high proportion of productive to non-productive activity was needed. The larger the market, the greater the scope for specialization and division of labour. He ascribed the value of a good to its labour input but its price to the interaction of supply and demand. Central to this analysis was the role of competition, by which, he believed, selfish individuals would be led to maximize the wellbeing of the whole of society. Therefore he advocated the minimum amount of government interference in the economic system.

Smith, A. (1970) *The Wealth of Nations*. Harmondsworth: Penguin.

socialism.   Covers a wide range of positions from communism to social democracy, all of which are against untrammelled capitalism.

Socialism first acquired governmental power in 1917. The first use of the word 'socialist' occurs in 1827 when it is used to describe the followers of Robert Owen, St Simon and Fourier, and socialism began in the heyday of Benthanism.

Communists, as a whole, would prefer to own and control the means of production, distribution and exchange to ensure fairer distribution of wealth, and often advocate a planned economy in an effort to make industry socially responsible. There is a danger that socialism is seen in nineteenth-century terms as a Marxist-Leninist philosophy, but this is to deny an older and different socialism: 'All Israel are brethren; and indeed there was a strange, antique clannishness about these Sons of the Covenant, which, in the modern world, where the ends of the ages meet, is Socialism' (Israel Zangwill, *Children of the Ghetto*, London, Dent, 1909).

Nowadays, western socialists opt for social democracy, and it is only in some developing countries that traditional socialist aims still prevail.

I welcome the rise of the Socialist Party in the Congress, but I can't say I like the programme as it appears in the printed pamphlet ... I do not like the assumption underlying many of its propositions ... which go to show that there is necessarily antagonism between the classes and the masses or between the labourers and capitalists, such that they can never work for mutual good' (Louis Fischer, *The Life of Mahatma Gandhi*, New York, Harper, 1950).

sound libraries. These have important uses in teaching history. As with **video**, the teacher is in control. The impact of an event like Martin Luther King's Civil Right's speech in 1963 is arguably greater without the distraction of the audience to whom he is speaking. A sound tape leaves more to the imagination.

Like most other approaches it is wise to respect certain rules: all the machinery must be set up beforehand; sound tapes should be easy to hear and not too scratchy or worn; the tapes and the machinery must be easy to use, and should not involve major classroom upheaval.

*See separate entry on **radio**.*

Annan Committee (1977).
Peacock Committee (1986).
Pilkington Committee (1962).

South-East Asia Treaty Organisation. SEATO was established under the South-East Asia Collective Defence Treaty of 1954 and signed in Manila. It was part of a general strategy by the USA to contain communism. The signatories were Australia, Britain, France, New Zealand, Pakistan, the Philippines, Thailand and the USA. The treaty covered South-East Asia and part of the south-west pacific. Pakistan and France withdrew from the Organisation in 1973 and 1974 respectively. The Organisation was dissolved in 1977 when communism was no longer a serious threat.

In many ways, SEATO was an attempt to reproduce NATO in the Pacific. However, the contexts for SEATO and NATO were very different. Each continent was different from the other, and so was the nature of the communism to which individual countries in Asia adhered. For most countries in SEATO, their communism was an independent communism. It was not a serious threat, nor was it a uniform political philosophy. China was powerful and united under Mao but it did not have the same control in Asia that the USSR and the Warsaw Pact had in Europe. There was no equivalent of the Warsaw Pact in the Far East, and the signatories to SEATO were even more diverse than the signatories to NATO.

Huxley, T. (1999) *Arming East Asia*. London: International Institute of Strategic Studies.

space. Travel beyond the Earth's atmosphere for the purpose of gathering information about space and other planets began in 1903 when the Russian, Kohstantin Tsiolkovsky, developed ideas for space rockets fuelled by liquid gas. By 1926 Robert Goddard of the USA had designed the first liquid-fuelled rocket. During the war, the Germans developed the V2 rocket. But it was the USSR which launched Sputnik I in 1957. This achievement had a huge impact on the USA, where it was followed, in 1958, with Explorer I. Then Yuri

Gagarin became, in 1961, the first man into space, followed by John Glenn in 1962. In 1969 Neil Armstrong and Buzz Aldrin landed on the moon. The USSR concentrated on unmanned flights, and Apollo IX achieved a soft landing on the moon in 1966. Then the USA and USSR started to co-operate and an Apollo capsule linked up with a Soviet Soyuz capsule in 1975. There have been unmanned flights to Venus, Mars, Neptune (through Voyager II, which was launched in 1977 and reached Neptune in 1989) and the launching of a space station, Mir, as well as the advent of the Hubble space telescope, both in 1990.

All these scientific developments have brought about an increased familiarity with outer space; improved global communications, through telecommunication satellites; and enhanced awareness of weather information and have enabled much to be learnt about the Earth's resources. They have also facilitated the collection of military information.

There is now the realization that political power is moving from governments and big corporations towards the individual. Is it conceivable that the collapse of communism was accelerated by the influence of personal computers and satellites? It is now impossible to prevent the spread of revolutionary ideas by a Berlin Wall, or some such other physical barrier.

Stalinism and Leninism. Lenin was responsible for significant amendments to Marx's ideology. He believed that the working class was only able to develop trade-union consciousness, whereas Marx had believed that the emancipation of the working class is the task the working class could be achieved by itself. Some Stalinists, therefore, believe Stalin's dictatorship was justified in order to extend the efforts of the working classes, which would not be enough by themselves.

Lenin believed in the organizational principle of democratic centralism which became a highly authoritarian structure and led inexorably to Stalinism.

It is said that Stalin destroyed rule through the Bolshevik Party. The core of the Bolsheviks had been swept away in the 1936–39 purges. Lenin's imperialism provided a justification for launching revolution in Russia in 1916. However, revolution did not sweep through Europe straight after the 1917 Russian Revolution because Lenin abandoned War Communism, the attempt to leap in one bound into a socialist economy. He envisaged the continuation of the New Economic Policy, or a mixed economy, for generations. By contrast, Stalin's ardent industrialization was the most dramatic discontinuity with Leninism and Bolshevism. So was Stalin's 'cult of personality'.

Lenin introduced the infamous 'ban on factions' in the 1921 Tenth Party Congress. This destroyed democratic centralism and was a stepping-stone to a climate of repression in the Party. Stalin physically destroyed the old Bolsheviks. But Lenin had created the system through which Stalin would rise. In that sense Stalin was the executor of Lenin's political will. Trotskyism and Bukharinism, though, arguably, equally legitimate, were outmanoeuvred by Stalin. 'Stalin destroyed crucial parts of the Leninist legacy ... and crossed the threshold from difference in degree to difference in kind' (Simm Hartree, 'Leninism versus Stalinism', *MHR*, **8**, November, 1996).

Nove, A. (ed.) (1993) *The Stalin Phenomenon*. London: Weidenfeld and Nicolson.
Volkagonov, D. (1994) *Lenin: Life and Legacy*. London: HarperCollins.

stamps. Collecting stamps is a way of arousing interest in history. Stamp collectors may specialize in any chosen area: national or international, biographies, major events or significant inventions. The attraction is often to the young, and collecting stamps is more practical as a hobby than many others. Stamps also look attractive; they are often well designed and colourful. They can also be a means of studying history without realizing it. 'All science is either physics or stamp collecting' (J. B. Birks, *Rutherford at Manchester*, Manchester University Press, 1962, p. 108).

Tosco, U. (1972) *Modern Stamps: Modern History in the Mail*. London: Orbis.

storytelling. Children like being told stories; consequently, stories are a 'winning ticket' as well as being a useful form of learning. They should be true, interesting and have a clear structure. Children will copy what they hear. Therefore, both language and content should be carefully prepared. Key names and phrases should be written as prompts, but the actual telling of the story is best done with headings rather than being written out in full. Like telling a joke, timing is critical and needs to be practised. 'A good story and a well-formed argument are different natural kinds. Both can be used as means for convincing another. Yet what they convince is fundamentally different: arguments convince of their truth, stories of the lifelikeness' (J. Bruner, *Actual Mind, Possible Worlds*, Harvard University Press, 1986, p. 11).

'The relationship between history and story has always been a difficult one: the very definition of story shifts along the uneven border between fact and fiction, between truth and lies, between emotional and causal logic' (C. Husbands, *What is History Teaching?* OUP, 1996, p. 46).

Farmer, A. (1990) 'Storytelling history'. *Teaching History*, **58**, January, 17–23.
Sampson, J. (1989) 'Storytelling in history'. *Teaching History*, **57**, October, 38.

study aids.   Books of notes, summaries of historical events, abridged documents and brief lives of the famous. They can save hours of note taking. They can supply the basic factual information, which can then form the basis of interpretation and analysis. They can be the framework into which an array of information can be fitted.

However, it can also be argued that avoiding making notes for oneself removes a valuable, perhaps essential, part of the learning and understanding of history. It is also argued that a set of printed notes provides a skeleton which, though easy to grasp, is not necessarily appropriate for the subject under consideration. Some subjects, for example the causes of the First World War, do not lend themselves readily to a codified list, compiled without in-depth reference to the subject. Conversely, it may also be better to carry the essential facts of a subject in one's head, because the interpretation of them can be obtained with the greatest ease. It is rather like a pianist who can perform with greater freedom once the notes of a piece have been memorized. But in history the facts that have to be grasped and memorized are better made by the person doing the interpretation.

Either way, it is essential that any study aid should be accurate and up to date; accurate, because the facts will be committed to memory, and up to date because the most recent account is often different from the earliest.

syllabus.   An outline of a course of study, in contrast to a curriculum which covers an entire set of subjects and cross-curricular activities. Examination syllabuses are now called specifications and are provided by awarding bodies, previously known as examination boards.

See separate entry on **National Curriculum**.

symbolism.   The practice of representation using symbols, or of giving a symbolic character to objects or acts. The swastika was a symbol of the Nazis, the cross of Christianity and the crescent of Islam. Hieroglyphs in Egypt are symbols, although it is not always clear what they represent. Fairy tales, folklore and mythologies are often symbolic, as they represent something other than themselves. An icon which is made to represent something holy or spiritual, as soon as it has been created seems to have an identity in its own right which can be equally holy and spiritual.

See separate entry on **emblems**.

Bayley, H. (1998) The Lost Language of Symbolism. London: Citadel.

T

telecommunications. Marx suggested that religion was 'the opium of the people'; it could be suggested that television is the current opium of the people. If this is the case then it is almost valueless in history teaching. The influence of television is so insidious that it must be handled with care and sensitivity in the classroom. Care, because it is such an overworked medium for so many children; and sensitivity, because if television is to have any impact it must be directed and focused. It is never enough to show a video and tell the children that they must 'make notes on the programme they are viewing'. First, interest must be aroused *before* the film is shown. It is often helpful to show a three-minute clip three or four times before showing a whole film. It is helpful to give a general preamble about the subject to be viewed and, at the same time, try to ensure that the 'bones' of the material are understood. It is usually helpful to ask questions either at the start or during a break. If the classroom lighting is good, then it is helpful to include some written work before the end so that it acts as a response to the film before it is finished.

Properly used, the medium is exciting.

Farmer, A. (1986) 'Video and history'. *TH*, **45**, June, 9–13.

terrorism. The practice of using violent and intimidating acts, especially for political ends. There are four main forms of terrorism: it can be organized by the state to suppress opposition; it can be sponsored *by* the state to encourage terrorist activities; it can bring pressure to bear on governments; and it can be used to overthrow a regime.

Whatever its form or expression, the objectives are usually clear: the intention is to keep a cause in the public eye and to cause a government to encourage or discourage a particular political stance. Terrorism has seldom succeeded in the long term, but it has often caused much suffering in the short term. The main techniques employed have included bombings and shootings, assassinations, hostage-taking and hi-jacking.

Examples of terrorism are diverse. In nineteenth-century Russia, anarchists and nihilists used bombings and assassinations against the tsarist government. In the USA, the Ku Klux Klan used lynchings and other savageries to intimidate black people. Mussolini and Hitler came to power partly by using terrorist tactics. Nationalist groups like the Palestine Liberation Organisation, have proliferated in Africa, Asia and the Middle East. There have also been powerful groups struggling against the regimes of their countries, and these have included the Baader-Meinhof Gang, the Red Army faction in Germany, the Red Brigades in Italy, *Action Directe* in France, the Basque Separatist groups in Spain, Tupamaros in Uruguay and Shining Palt in Peru.

International action against terrorism has not been very effective, in spite of the introduction, in 1977, of the European Convention on the Suppression of Terrorism, the Trevi system in EU member states in 1976 and the Tokyo Summit declaration on terrorism in 1986. Nevertheless, tighter airport security and laws on extradition have both proved difficult to arrange.

time.   Piaget held that the three stages of space, time and causality were the three stages of child development. Therefore, the relevance of particular stages in the way a child learns is very important and the teacher must pitch the story appropriately. History taught in the pre-adolescent years should be as concrete as possible. Michael Sturt (1925) claimed that many children had

> no organization of the past … he relegates whatever seems to him to be beyond his own experience, or the possible experience of those to whom he comes into close contact to the dim regions of savagery. As a result teacher expectation must be tailored to suit the intellectual potential of the children involved.'

In short, do not expect children to have an appreciation of time when they are not sufficiently mature in years.

See separate entry on **chronology**.

Jahoda, G. (1963) 'Children's concept of time and history'. *Education Review*, 15 February.
Peel, E. A. (1967) *Studies in the Nature and Teaching of History*. London: Routledge.
Sturt, M. (1925) *The Psychology of Tune*. London: Kegan Paul.
Teaching History (1991) **62**, January.
Teaching History (1995) **81**, October.

toys.   For the historian, toys can represent one point in time. Some toys, such as dolls' houses, represent particular architectural or furniture styles. The Museum of Childhood, formerly the Bethnal Green Museum, is a branch of the Victoria and Albert Museum. It contains a collection of dolls' houses, dolls, model furniture, toys, children's books and children's costumes.

See separate entry under **museums (London)**.

Tonge, N. (1995) 'Toys: a living history for Key Stage One'. *TH*, October.

transport.   Towns were often built on rivers; empires and states have been shaped by transport possibilities and limitations from Roman times to the present day. Transport was also an important part of the Industrial Revolution; the development of roads, turnpikes, the internal combustion engine, canals and barges and railways were all critical developments during the eighteenth and nineteenth centuries. You cannot have heavy industry – coal, wool and cotton – without also having associated means of transport. But transport has a much wider context than just the Industrial Revolution. The invention of the wheel transformed society, and the subsequent development of carts, trolleys and water wheels continued the quiet revolution. The wheel disturbed the enclosed village economy more than any other single factor.

Trams first appeared in Birkenhead in 1860, and by 1880, 233 miles of tramways had been constructed in England and Wales. They made a major contribution to the development of cities like Manchester, Newcastle and Sheffield, and in all of these they have now been reinstated.

Other vehicles were also significant: the bicycle, the motor car and the underground train had major effects. In addition, the development of flight, from the early years of the twentieth century onwards, dominated society in peacetime and in wartime. The first manned space flight took place in 1961. Ships, boats and submarines complete the array. Since humans began to move freely, transport has been intrinsic to the culture of modern life.

Boughey, J. (1998) *Hadfield's Canals*. London: Budding.
Lobley, D. (1973) *Ships Through the Ages*. London: Octopus Books.
Woodman, R. (1997) *History of the Ship*. London: Conway.

U

uniform. The idea of wearing the same clothes, or having distinguishing clothing has long been a characteristic of humans. Certain distinctive groups, such as the Brown Shirts in Fascist Italy, or the Black Shirts in Nazi Germany, wished to be seen as belonging to a tightly organized group. In other areas, e.g. the Roman Catholic Church, monks and nuns were also to be distinguished by a uniform, and the formal clothing of Religious was a major and significant step on the religious journey of the individuals concerned.

In Nazi Germany Jews had to wear the Star of David, often with the word 'JUDEN' written across the back of their garment, and homosexuals had to wear a pink triangle.

One of the most helpful (and easy) ways of incorporating uniforms into history is to suggest that any project should include newspaper or magazine pictures showing the uniform of the time. Since photographs started to be produced, and reproduced, over 100 years ago, there are now enough supplies to satisfy the most voracious collecting appetites. A photograph of uniformed soldiers in the trenches of Flanders in the 1914–18 war, with their puttees, old helmets and old rifles, greatly aids verbal explanation, as well as being an essential part of the account of the war.

United Nations. An international organization intended to secure world peace and security. It was intended to replace the League of Nations, and founded at a conference in San Francisco in 1945. Fifty nations signed the Charter. The UN consists of a General Assembly of all members and an inner core of the Security Council – the USA, Soviet Union (now Russia), National China (since 1971) (now People's Republic of China), Britain and France. Each has the right of veto.

The UN is based in New York and there are a wide range of

organizations associated with it, e.g. UNESCO, UNHCR (UN High Commission for Refugees) and the International Court of Justice.

UNESCO Sourcebook:

Maddison, J. (1986) *The Unesco and Britain Dossier 1945–1986*, Museums and Archives Development Associates.
UNESCO (1979) List of Documents and Publications. Paris: Unesco.

United Nations Charter:

Bourantonis, D. and Wiener, J. (eds) (1995) *The United National in the New World Order: The World Organization at Fifty*. Basingstoke: Macmillan.
Lister, F. (1996) *The European Union, The United Nations and the Revival of Confederal Governance*. Westport, CT: Greenwood Press.
Luard, E. (1978) *The United Nations*. London: Macmillan.
Simma, B. (ed.) (1994) *A Commentary*. Oxford: OUP.
UN Centre for Disarmament Affairs (1996). *The United Nations and Disarmament since 1945*. New York: UN.

United States of America.   The USA has a population of over 265 million (1996 figures), covers 3,679,192 square miles and, militarily, is the most powerful nation in the world. The thirteen colonies declared independence from Britain on 4 July 1776 and, at the end of the War of Independence, the Peace of Paris in 1783 recognized the independence of the United States. The 1787 constitution set out the structure of a federal system with a central government and constituent states, an executive president and two houses in the legislature. The Senate consisted of two senators from each state, and the House of Representatives comprised Congress members, elected from constituencies of equal size. The independent judiciary is headed by the Supreme Court.

The new country expanded with the Louisiana Purchase in 1803 and the acquisition of Florida in 1810–19. Texas and California were acquired as result of the Mexican–American War of 1846–48.

The American Civil War of 1861–5 was about the rights states should possess, e.g. slavery and stopping permanent secession of the southern states. The Civil War caused much pain and suffering but, in the end, unified the nation. Alaska was purchased in 1867 and Spanish overseas territories were acquired as part of the settlement of the Spanish–American War of 1898.

The USA fought in both world wars, in spite of powerful isolationism. The USA has been a member of the United Nations since its foundation in 1945. It has fought in the Korean War and the Vietnam War and has intervened in several South American and Caribbean countries when it looked as if extreme left-wing groups were gaining control.

Prominent in the Cold War, the USA has subsequently helped to resolve regional disputes and has participated in United Nations peace-keeping operations.

See separate entries on **American democracy; presidents of the USA**; **slave trade and slavery**.

Andrews, W. (1963) *Concise Dictionary of American History*. Oxford: OUP.
Cooke, A. (1973) *America*. London: Random House.
Rappaport, A. (1966) *Sources in American Diplomacy*. London: Collier-Macmillan.

Union of Soviet Socialist Republics (1922–91).

The USSR was named at a congress of the first four republics in 1922. Government was based on the national ownership of land and means of production, with legislative power in the hands of the Supreme Soviet. Collectivization of agriculture transformed the country. Over 20 million people died during the Stalinist period. Foreign policy had become a powerful weapon by 1939 with the signing of the Nazi–Soviet Pact. In addition, the USSR, by 1936, was composed of fifteen constituent republics. Soon Poland was annexed (in conjunction with Germany); the Baltic States were annexed in 1939 and Finland was invaded. However, there was a different result when Germany invaded Soviet Russia in 1941 because the latter changed sides and joined the Allies. The USSR eventually declared war on Japan in 1945.

Soviet Russia was prominent at the peace conferences in Teheran, Yalta and Potsdam, and joined the United Nations. Russia created the tight block of eastern European countries, on the USSR's initiative, through the Warsaw Pact, a defensive alliance to counterbalance **NATO**. Soviet troops were sent to Hungary and Poland in 1956, and to Czechoslovakia in 1968 when liberal programmes in those countries began to challenge the Soviet-inspired nature of the governments concerned.

Although relations with China deteriorated in the 1950s, the Soviet Union helped pro-Soviet governments. Afghanistan was invaded in 1979 and a pro-Soviet government was installed. It signed the Helsinki Agreement on **human rights**. Mikhail Gorbachev was elected Secretary-General in 1985 and the country entered a new period of openness and liberalization (see separate entry on **glasnost and perestroika**). As a result there were demands for independence from the republics which made up the USSR. The Soviet Union collapsed in December 1991. Many of the constituent countries became independent and have now joined an alliance called the Commonwealth of Independent States.

Lane, D. (1985) *Soviet Economy and Society*. Oxford: Blackwell.
Nove, A. (1969) *An Economic History of the USSR*. London: Allen Lane.
Pares, B. (1962) *History of Russia*. London: Cape.

V

---

video. A magnetic tape suitable for recording pictures and sound. A topic can be effectively introduced, summarized or highlighted. It can enable double projection, in order to look at part of a larger picture in more detail.

BBC Educational Publishing PO Box 234, Wetherby, West Yorks LS23 7EU.
BBC Education Information, White City, 201 Wood Lane, London W12 7TS.
Channel 4, 124 Horseferry Road, London SW1P 2TX.
Granada Television, Granada TV Centre, Quay Street, Manchester M60 9EA.
ITV Association, Knighton House, 56 Mortimer Street, London W1N 2AN.

Vietnam. Previously French Indo-China and decolonized under General de Gaulle in July 1954. The communist government in the north, under Ho Chi Minh, started to infiltrate the south. The USA feared that South Vietnam would become communist and, towards the end of John F. Kennedy's presidency, sent 'military advisers' and combat troops in readiness for conflict. Eventually, guerilla war broke out and increasing numbers of American troops fought to bolster South Vietnam. After much hand-to-hand fighting the war ended in April 1975 when North Vietnamese forces captured Saigon, the capital of South Vietnam, and renamed it Ho Chi Minh City in 1976.

The war was controversial and of great importance for several reasons: it was the first televised war; it was probably the biggest conflict of the Cold War era; it was accentuated, if not provoked, by the Domino Theory, which suggested that one state after another in the Far East would become communist unless the drift to communism was stopped; it was strongly opposed in the United States by significant numbers of people, but President Johnson had been given congressional approval to take military action, and by 1967, 400,000 men from the USA were serving in Vietnam with military support from Australia, New Zealand and Thailand; it became a rallying point for left-wing opinion throughout the world in support of North Vietnam, and in the UK there were large demonstrations in Grosvenor Square, outside the US Embassy, in 1967 and 1968; it became a major problem for Harold Wilson who refused to support America in any way, but was also unwilling to condemn the war, thereby arousing criticism from all sides including his own party and precipitating the growth of radical left-wing groups.

The harsh truth for the USA was that they lost the war. They lost many citizens as well. They did not stop the spread of communism in the Far East. They challenged the time-honoured Anglo-American Alliance and, as a result, lost face and credibility.

Teaching this subject today is likely to be influenced by a spate of American films about the war. Some are worth showing, to illustrate the harsh nature of the fighting and the biased nature of the accounts portrayed. Savage though most of the films are, they are worth showing on video, allowing frequent pauses for group discussion. Points to highlight are the savagery of war, the nature of communism, the power of bias and propaganda and the self-interest of American military involvement.

virtual history.   Part of what is called 'virtual reality', which is a 3-D interactive space, generated by a computer for projection on a hand-mounted display, or on a standard computer screen. It is a way of encouraging an enquiry into history or immersion in the past. It enables children to be taken to places which have historical significance, but is not a substitute for field trips. A visit is composed of what is seen, whereas virtual history allows the student 'to manipulate historical variables and explore speculative questions' (Pluchrose, 1991).

Bruner, J. S. (1974) *Beyond the Information Given*. London: Unwin.
Grove, J. (1996) *Virtual History, History and Computing*, Vol. 8, No.1. Edinburgh: Edinburgh University Press.
Pluchrose, H. (1991) *Children Learning History*. Oxford: Blackwell Education.

voting systems.   An attempt to express the way people think. All of the existing systems have strong advocates in all the political parties. The five main systems are:

'First-past-the-post': the current method of electing members to the House of Commons. It is also used in the USA, Canada and India. Each voter votes for one candidate and the candidate with the most votes is elected. However, if the votes for all the other candidates are added together it often reveals that the winner does not have an overall majority.

The single transferable vote (STV) is for voting for candidates, not for parties. Voters put the candidates in order, 1, 2, 3, and then the total number of first preferences are counted. The total is divided by the number of seats, plus one, to produce a quota. To be elected, a candidate's votes must reach the same number as the quota. If the voter's first-choice candidate does not need their vote because he or she is already elected, or has too few votes, then the vote is transferred to the voter's second-choice candidate, and so on. This method means that the party need not be so dominant in an election, because other candidates in different parties might receive some second or third votes. It is the system used in Australia, Eire, Tasmania, Malta and Northern Ireland in local and European elections.

The Additional Member System (AMS) is a mixed system combing first-past-the-post with party-list voting. Each voter has two votes, one for a single MP in the constituency and a second for a regional or national-party constituency. Half the seats are allocated to the single-member constituencies and the other half to the party list. This system is used in Germany, New Zealand, Scotland (for the Scottish Parliament) and Wales (for the Welsh Assembly).

Party lists are used in Israel, and were used in Europe for the first time in the British European elections in 1999. Instead of voting in constituencies, electors vote for a party in a multi-member constituency, regionally or nationwide. When the votes are counted, a quota is calculated for the constituency – the number of votes required to win one seat. Those who become the party's MPs will be those placed highest in the party's list of candidates.

The Alternative Vote system is used in Australia to elect the House of Representatives. Instead of voting for a single candidate, the voter puts candidates in order of preference. The one with the majority of first votes is elected. However, if no single candidate gets more than 50 per cent of the vote, the candidate with the least first preferences is eliminated and his or her second preferences are then added to the votes of the remaining candidates, and so on until one candidate has at least 50 per cent of the vote.

Frank Field, in a letter to *The Times* (14 August 1999), wrote:

> No amount of arguing is going to convince voters that redistributing the second-preference votes of losers, and giving those votes the same value as first preference votes, will build a fairer electoral system. Voters are more likely to share Winston Churchill's view that an electoral system allowing candidates to be elected on second-preference votes is one in which 'the decision is to be determined by the most worthless votes given for the most worthless candidates'.

An article in *The Times* (26 October 1999) by Peter Riddell included the emotive phrase: 'The real doubt is whether the coalitions produced by PR are workable.'

Further detailed information can be obtained from the Electoral Reform Society, 6 Chancel Street, Blackfriars, London SE1 0UU. Tel: 0207 928 1622.

A good way for students to understand the systems is for them to run a series of mock elections themselves. Then the systems, which seem rather complicated when described, or on paper, become altogether easier to comprehend.

The latest report in Britain is by the Jenkins Commission, available from HMSO.

W

war studies.   It includes the following sub-headings: air, land and sea warfare; internal revolutions (the English Civil War, French, American, Russian and Chinese); **guerrilla** war; and espionage.

See separate entry on **World Wars I and II**.

Andrew, C. and Noakes, J. (1987) *Intelligence and International Relations 1900–1945*. Exeter: Exeter University.
Melton, H. K. (1996) *The Ultimate Spy Book*. London: Dorling Kindersley.

women's history.   The National Curriculum states that there should be included 'the experiences of men and women' to ensure a balance in the treatment of history and this must be addressed at every stage.

See separate entry on **gender**.

Beddoe, D. (1983) *Discovering Women's History*. London: Pandora.
Booth, M. (1983) 'Sex differences and historical understanding'. *TH*, **36**, June, 7–8.
Boulding, E. (1981) *The Underside of History: A View of Women Through Time*. London: Westview Press.
Coss, P. (1998) *The Lady in Medieval England*. London: Wrens Park.
Holland, J., Blair, M., Sheldon, S. (eds) (1995) *Debates and Issues in Feminist Research and Pedagogy*. Clevedon, Avon: Multilingual Matters.
Hufton, Olwen *et al.* (1985) 'What is Women's History?' *History Today*, **35**, June, 38–48.
Moorse, K. (1992) *Genderwatch!* (ed. K. Myers). Cambridge: CUP.
National Women's History Project (Women's Rights Movement 1848–1998) – website: http://www.legacy98.org (contains the most recent material).
Wellbourne, D. (1990) 'Women's history through local history'. *TH*, **59**, April, 16–21. website: http:/frank.mtsu.edu/-kmiddlet/history/women/women in.html (this is an index site which is constantly updated).

world history.   The syllabus for a world history course is either based on samples from the five continents (making India a sub-continent and dividing America into north and south, making a total of eight); or examples are taken from a contrasted range of individual countries. The aim of such structures is to contain as many different variants of ethnicity, employment, population patterns, wars (including terrorism), imperialism and territorial aggression as possible.

In sourcing material, particularly for recent history, the cultural departments of the foreign embassies are usually very helpful.

The International Baccalaureate history syllabus tackles these major logistical problems and contains well-tried programmes. Schools of all kinds take this exam, but there is strong participation from international schools where the IB seeks to service the diverse needs of pupils coming from different countries who need to obtain a qualification which is acceptable when they return.

The essential question is whether a syllabus based on a wide and diversified geographical area can be a feasible examination project. The essential answer is that the study of the particular subjects chosen must be as rigorous and as detailed as it would be if the syllabus was narrower in scope. There is, for example, no valid reason why slavery in the eighteenth century in Africa or the Caribbean could not be studied in detail as seriously as studying a series of documents concerning one plantation in Tennessee; the emphasis is on the learning skills in both examples, not on the breadth or the narrowness of the geographical area chosen; but the documentary evidence must be comparable for both analyses to be acceptable.

Dockmill, M. (1991) *Atlas of Twentieth Century World History*. London: Collins.
HMSO (1967) *Towards World History* (Educational Pamphlet 52). London: HMSO.
Philips Atlas of World History (1999). London: Philips.
Times Atlas of World History (1997). London: *Times* Books.

world religions.   Historians should explain the history and customs of major world religions. The main religions are:

Hinduism: the world's oldest living religion; there are 500 million followers today.

Judaism: the Jewish faith; there are 14 million Jews.

Buddhism: followers of Buddha; there are over 500 million today.

Christianity: followers of Jesus Christ; there are over 1000 million. It is the largest religion in the world.

Islam: God's word was revealed to Mohammed in the seventh century. He became a prophet of God. There are about 1000 million followers of Islam.

Sikhism: founded about 1500 by Guru Nanak. There are 12 million Sikhs.

Meredills, S. (1995) *World Religions*. London: Usborne Publishing.

World Wars I (1914–18) and II (1939–45). The two world wars have dominated the twentieth century and have involved many countries in the world and all the countries of Europe.

In 1941 the Allied Powers were Britain, France, Russia, Japan and Serbia. They were joined by Italy in 1915, Portugal and Romania in 1916 and the USA and Greece in 1917. They fought Germany, Austro-Hungary, Turkey and Bulgaria. The war was fought on the Western Front, on the Eastern Front, in Mesopotamia, Palestine, north-east Italy and in the German colonies in Africa and the Pacific. The Versailles settlement was the formal end to the war. Casualties in this war were enormous, partly caused because both sides thought that superiority of numbers would prevail. Tragically, prolonged trench war, with consequent massive loss of life, was a feature of the conflict.

The 1939–45 war was between the Allies (Britain, the USSR and the USA) and the Axis (Germany, Italy and, eventually, Japan). It started in Europe when Britain, rejecting an earlier policy of appeasement towards Germany, declared war on 3 September 1939, following Hitler's invasion of Poland. War broke out in many European countries and Nazi Germany seemed in control of much of the continent, until Hitler invaded Soviet Russia, which proved to be a turning point, even though his armies reached the outskirts of Moscow. He had to retreat when the Russians defeated the German army at Kirsk and Stalingrad. In 1942 the first allied counter-offensive began in North Africa and moved to Italy. The Allied landings in Normandy started in June 1944 and Germany surrendered in May 1945 after Hitler had committed suicide.

The only significant naval battle in the First World War had been at Jutland in 1916. There was, however, many more naval conflicts in the Second World War. When Japan attacked the US fleet at Pearl Harbor in December 1941, the USA not only entered the war on the side of the Allies but fought as much at sea as on land.

Air power developed from reconnaissance to bombing in the 1914–18 war, and also included fighter combat. Air power was more crucial in the 1939–45 war and involved massive bombing raids by both Germany and Britain.

The Great Wars PC CD-ROM A674 – www.times.reader offer.co.uk

website: First World War (Spartacus schoolnet) – http:// www.spartacus.schoolnet.co.uk/ FWWtitle.html (a history of the First World War, written by people from different countries)

website: Information on the History of World War II – http://history.hanover.edu/20th/ wwii.htm

website: The trenches – http://world war 1.com/reflib.htm

York Castle Museum.   The Museum is housed in two converted prisons joined by a concourse. It contains collections which recreate the atmosphere of everyday life during the past 300 years – crafts, costumes, toys and technology – and all in a recreated street with shops that are open to view.

There are special facilities for teachers of multi-curricular studies in the National Curriculum and clear instructions and help is provided for teachers leading parties, which should be no larger than 50.

In history, the displays are as follows:

KS1   A vivid impression of everyday life from 1770 to 1990
KS2   Study Unit 3a: Victorian Britain
      Study Unit 3b: Britain since 1930, which covers the impact of the Second World War
KS3   Study Unit 2: The English Civil War as it relates to Yorkshire
      Study Unit 3: Artefacts giving evidence for growth of trade and industrial production
      Study Unit 4: Currently (1999/2000) the Second World War

The Museum is only one of the many treasures York has to offer. George VI said: 'The history of York is the history of England.' Other major features include York Minster, the York Story (in St Mary's Castlegate), the Yorkshire Museum, Clifford's Tower (motte-and-bailey in origin), the Railway Museum, the Yorvik Viking Centre, various Guild Halls of the medieval and modern craft companies, the Treasurer's House, St William's College, the Art Gallery, the Military Museum, the Manor House, the Guildhall and Terry's chocolate factory.

York Castle Museum, The Eye of York, York YO1 9RY. Tel: 0345

660280 (information); 01904 653611 (general enquiries); 01904 633932 (group bookings to be made in advance); website: http://www.york.gov.uk

Z

Zaibatsu. Zaibatsu is the prewar Japanese word for industrial conglomerates. After the war, the US abolished these Zaibatsu, held together by a common company in each grouping, fearing they had been a major reason why Japan had started war with China, in 1937, and with the US, Britain and Australia in 1941. Although they were powerful influences they were not responsible directly for formal education, which was the business of the state. Compulsory, full-time state education was seen as the key to national economic growth, financial security and the creation of a system of improved social status based on merit by examination. The Zaibatsu accepted gratefully the products of such education, who were literate, conformist and hard-working. The powerful influences of the over-arching Zaibatsu were more discrete, but nevertheless intrinsic to the whole perspective.

Rote learning in history and all other subjects, though unimaginative, served to provide a common basis for shared national awareness. It was believed that learning historical and other facts without challenging the underlying assumptions was not far removed from learning commercial and industrial practices, though such a bold claim would not have been expressed. It was tacitly understood that there would be an easy transference from the classroom to the office or to the factory, and this was deemed to lead to the ultimate industrial efficiency. Thus, unobtrusively, Zaibatsu helped to build, and then shape, the nation. They embraced the educational common denominator and produced numerate, literate and educated men and women, though Zaibatsu did not actually run the educational system. They are now more usually known in Japan as Keiretsu.

Amano, Y. (1990) *Education and Examination in Modern Japan*. Tokyo: Tokyo University Press.
Cummings, W. K. (1980) *Education and Equality in Japan*. Princeton, NJ: Princeton University Press.

Zwingli. Huldrych Zwingli (1484–1531) was a Swiss Protestant reformer. He was influenced by **Erasmus**. He came to Zurich and preached that the Church should return to the simple beliefs and practices of the New Testament. Priests began to marry, fasts were disregarded and images were destroyed. Zwingli thought the Church consisted of the people. Some of the Swiss Cantons (see **federal**) followed Zwingli; others remained faithful to Rome. Then religious war broke out in which Zwingli was killed.

Gabler, U. (1986) *Huldrych Zwingli*. London: Fortress.

List of Headwords

Advanced Level

aerial photography

affective learning

Agrarian or Agricultural Revolution

American democracy

American Historical Association

American Museum Bath

anthropology

archaeology

archives

architecture

art

Asian history

assessment

Association of History and Computing

astrology

astronomy

atlas

Attainment Targets

Australia

Australian Historical Association

baccalauréat

balance of power

Bath Museum of Costume

Bayeux Tapestry

Bede

bias and prejudice

Bible in English

biography and autobiography

Black Power movement in the USA

British Library

British Museum

Bruner

Calvin

Canada

Canadian Catholic Historical Association

Canadian Historical Association

cartoons

castles

cathedrals

celibate

Central Office of Information

Certificate of Achievement

Certificate of Secondary Education

Charlemagne

Chata project

children

Christianity

chronology

churches and chapels

citizenship

classroom aids, apparatus and materials

cognitive domain

comics

communism

compact disc-read only memory

concept

conservation

contemporary history

costume

countryside

county record offices

curriculum

Darwin

Dearing Report and Review

debating

differentiation

documents

drama

emblem

empathy

English Heritage

list of headwords

South-East Asia Treaty Organisation

space

Stalinism and Leninism

stamps

storytelling

study aids

syllabus

symbolism

telecommunications

terrorism

time

toys

transport

uniform

United Nations

United States of America

Union of Soviet Socialist Republics

videos

Vietnam

virtual history

voting systems

war studies

women's history

world history

world religions

World Wars I and II

York Castle Museum

Zaibatsu

Zwingli

List of Organizations

ACCAC   Awdurdod Cymwysterau, Cwricwlwn ac Asesu Cymru
           Castle Buildings, Womanby Street, Cardiff CF1 9SX
           Tel: 029 203 75400.

AQA   The Assessment and Qualifications Alliance
           comprising AEB/SEG, CITY AND GUILDS, NEAB
           Addleshaw Booth & Co., Sovereign House, PO Box 8,
           Sovereign Street, Leeds LS1 1HQ Tel: 0161 953 7527.

CCEA   Council for the Curriculum, Examinations and
           Assessment
           Clarendon Dock, 29 Clarendon Road, Belfast BT1
           3BG Tel: 028 902 61200.

DfEE   Department for Education and Employment
           Sanctuary Buildings, Great Smith Street, London
           SW1P 3BT Tel: 0870 001 2345.

DENI   Department for Education, Northern Ireland
           Raltgael House, Balloo Road, Bangor, County Down
           BT18 7PR Tel: 028 91 279 100.

OFSTED   Office for Standards in Education
           Alexandra House, 33 Kingsway, London WC2B 6SE
           Tel: 0207 421 6800.

QCA   Qualifications and Curriculum Authority
           29 Bolton Street, London W1Y 7PD Tel: 0207 509
           5555.

SCCC   Scottish Consultative Council on the Curriculum
           Gardyne Road, Broughty Ferry, Dundee DD5 1NY
           Tel: 01382 443 600.

SOEID   Scottish Office Education and Industry Department
Victoria Quay, Leith, Edinburgh EH6 6QQ Tel: 0131
477 2780.

WOEED   Welsh Office Education Department
Government Buildings, Cathays Park, Cardiff CF1
3NQ Tel: 0292 082 5111.

For environmental organizations see separate entry on the **countryside.**

Bibliography

Butler, A. (1993) *A Dictionary of Dates*. London: Dent.

Cannon, J. (ed.) (1997) *Oxford Companion to British History*. Oxford: OUP.

Childrens Books in Print: A Reference Catalogue. London: Whitaker (revised bi-annually).

A Dictionary of Historical Slang (1972). Harmondsworth: Penguin.

Encyclopedia of World History (1998). Oxford: OUP.

Gardiner, J. and Wenboon, N. (eds) (1995) *The History Today Companion to British History*. London: Collins and Brown.

Honderich, T. (ed.) (1995) *Oxford Companion to Philosophy*. Oxford: OUP.

Roberts, J. M. (1999) *Twentieth Century: The History of the World 1901 to the Present*. Harmondsworth: Allen Lane.

Journals and Publications Quoted

AHC	Journal of the Association of History and Computing
AHR	Agricultural History Review
BECTa	British Educational Communications and Technology Agency
BIHR	Bulletin of the Institute of Historical Research
BJSE	British Journal of Special Education
CJ	Curriculum Journal
DNB	Dictionary of National Biography
EcHR	Economic History Review
EHR	English Historical Review
GEM	Group for Education in Museums Journal
H	History
HA	Historical Association
HJ	Historical Journal
HT	History Today
IHR	Institute of Historical Research Journal
LH	The Local Historian
MH	Midland History

bibliography

MHR	Modern History Review
MJ	Museums Journal
NH	Northern History
NT	National Trust Magazine
SHR	Scottish Historical Review
SocH	Social History Journal
TH	Teaching History
TRHS	Transactions of the Royal Historical Society
VCH	Victoria County History